The All of Everything

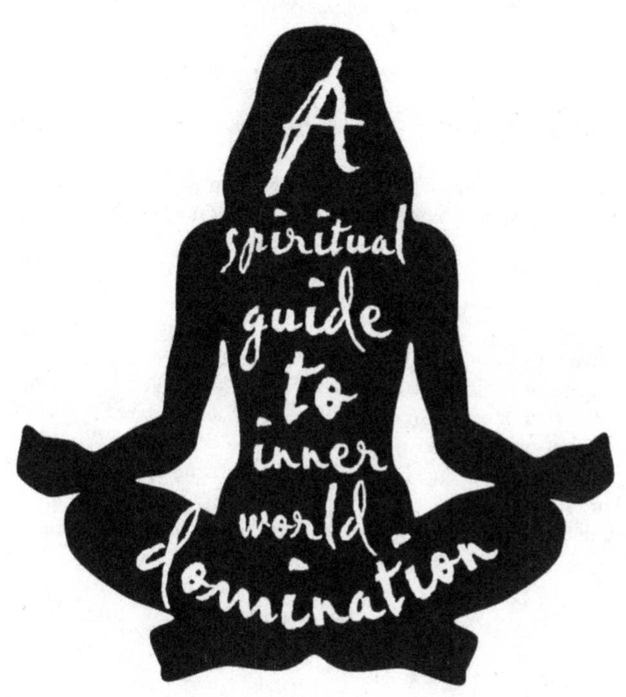

LAURA SALTMAN

The All of Everything:
A Spiritual Guide to Inner World Domination

ISBN: 978-1-948443-00-5 (print), 978-1-948443-01-2 (epub)

DISCLAIMER

The information and opinions expressed here are believed to be accurate based on the best judgement available to the author. This book is intended to be educational, as a means to guide you on your spiritual journey. The author of this book does not dispense medical advice or prescribe the use of any technique as a form of treatment for physical, emotional or medical problems without the advice of a physician or medical professional. In the event you use any of the information in this book for yourself, the author and the publisher assume no responsibility for your actions.

Cover by Wendy Kis

For my dad and brother.

In their deaths was my true purpose revealed.

In my sorrow did the voice within begin speaking to me.

May we journey through lifetimes together, always.

Preface

If you are reading this book, I know you have been guided here because you too are searching for answers and have prayed either consciously or subconsciously for help. Perhaps you need to hear it from someone like me—someone who is neither a spiritual guru nor a person who has had any particular religious background before embarking on this spiritual journey, someone who doesn't even like the word "God."

Plenty of people have proclaimed (or at least quietly admitted) that they speak to God on the regular. Some have even written books or essays about it. I am not the first, nor will I be the last. I am just bold (and perhaps stupid!) enough to want to share my conversation with the masses.

It bears noting that this book was written by someone with no reference point to the Gospel, Torah, or other religious-based material. I believe this is precisely why I was the perfect conduit for writing it. Telling friends, family, and strangers about how this book came to be and how I "talk to God" makes even me laugh. Though I had been studying spiritual principles and was told by a medium I was an intuitive and a channel, the whole thing still seemed absolutely ludicrous.

It wasn't until I finally comprehended, through the writing of this book, we are all part of an energy system and are never separated from this source, that I truly understood to whom I was actually talking. It is all of us together. We are one mind. We are cocreators. God is not some figurehead in the clouds, it is the energy of the universe, a collective conscious which split itself into individual consciousness's for the purposes of growing and evolving the soul. "God" is just the word we use to name the unnamable.

God. Universe. Source. Spirit. These are the words many spiritual teachers use. As hard as it was for me, I use the word God in the book because I felt guided to—until I was given the title of this book: *The All of Everything*. This is what we all are. I believe some spiritual teachers also use the word "God" because it's easier and appeals more to the masses. God, I believe, would prefer to be called "I Am," or just "Love" but because God said "God" would help more people, "God" it is. It's easier than grasping the concept of being part of an all-encompassing, all-knowing, all-loving energy system. Plus, our world has shown that it loves to worship famous people. It's my job to interview celebrities, and who is more famous than God?

Up until recently, writing a book wasn't even in my thoughts, especially not a book that would require me to constantly tell people how I interviewed "God." I always wanted to be an entertainment reporter. "I don't want to be a star; I want to interview the stars," I would say. Well, I guess that came true in more ways than one.

This whole book came to be, in July 2017, because I had recently begun listening to the best-selling book series *Conversations with God*.[1] The series is written by Neale Donald Walsch, a man who proclaimed to speak to God. Walsch's books had zero religious undertones and were practical in nature; they were right up my nonreligious alley. Walsch said we all have the ability within ourselves to communicate with God and that we can tap into that ability for guidance. I thought in my journaling that perhaps I was already doing this on paper but wasn't quite sure. "Could I do such a thing too?" I wondered. Could I actually hear the voice of God?

One particularly hot summer evening I couldn't sleep, so I turned on my computer and started typing questions about my life. Sure enough, as quickly as I typed a question, an answer came to me (just as Walsch said it had for him) in my head. My spirit voice within tuned into my channel almost immediately.

At first, my questions were of a personal nature, and the responses were simplistic. I initially thought it could have been just me responding using what I already knew of spiritual principle. However, something incredible began to happen as the questions went more in-depth. It became a conversation that was absolutely otherworldly.

Once I read what I had written back to myself, I knew I wasn't coming up with the answers. As crazy as it sounds, and trust me it's crazy to me, I can't deny the truth—this book wrote itself. I was not capable of such consistency and clarity, nor was I capable of writing so easily and effortlessly. Vocabulary I never used, nor even knew the definition of, flowed out of me. Thoughts were translated instantaneously with no lag time as I wrote.

I quickly learned how to differentiate between my voice and the Spirit within. My voice (the ego) is loud; it sounds like me, and it comes from the top right of my head. The Spirit voice is much quieter (almost a whisper); it has no real quality to its tone, and it comes from the back right of my head.

Like a good journalist would, I questioned everything, especially when ideas went against my personal beliefs. What was astounding was that I was writing things I had never heard of (or at the time could comprehend) in any of the spiritual books or material I had encountered. The Spirit voice made shocking revelations about how our thoughts affect not only us but also those around us. "All minds connected, all minds responsible," it told me.

The Spirit voice turned common phrases on their heads. "In God we trust" became "Of God we trust." It shed light on current events and explained or debunked historical and theological ideas. It referenced periods of history that I knew nothing about, including the Tiananmen Square massacre and even the story of Adam and Eve.

My hands were guided to type quotation marks around certain words or put them in bold or italics. Sometimes I would erase a sentence or word only to rewrite it, almost as if I were fighting with God. I always gave in.

The best way I can explain how this book came to be is that God is within each and everyone of us. When we are totally aware of Love's presence in our lives, our energetic vibration is at a frequency where we can hear the words spoken through us. The best way to hear this inner dialogue is in quiet meditation. For me, meditation was typing alone at my computer. My channel opened, and I was able to hear and connect with Spirit.

Is it worth risking my professional reputation that I spent twenty years building to share this material? Absolutely. If Theresa Caputo of *The Long Island Medium*, with her big hair and Long Island accent, can share how she talks to dead people, then this entertainment reporter can certainly suck it up and explain how she talked to God. Though you may find it hard to believe, every time you read here that I did talk to God, you should know that you can too because God is inside each and every one of us.

I want to make it clear that what you will read in the interview was a dictation, sort of like what a stenographer sitting in a court room would take. I wrote what I heard as fast as I could. In spiritual terms, it would be called "automatic writing." Many healers and spiritual teachers have undertaken this with spirit energies. Many more may be inspired to try this from reading this very book, as *Conversations with God* did for me.

Also note that I made the conscious choice to not edit any of the dialogue. Every time I read this interview back to myself, I prayed about the material to be sure I didn't include anything stemming from the ego (irrational) mind. As it was dictated to me is exactly how it remains.

There are some incredibly radical notions in this book that are very much at war with how I think and believe and likely with how much of those (who have yet to unravel or be reminded of their spiritual nature) thinks and believes. I did, however, find it necessary to release the fear about presenting it this way, as I also believe the information provided is truthful and accurate.

The repetitive nature of the text is purposeful as well. For this is how we truly learn. Until I fully recognized and understood an idea, Spirit persisted in making its points. And the truth is that the principles are always the same; they are just told in a different way. So most of the time the answer will be the same. I barely understood some of what was being revealed to me, which is why you will find my questions are of a repetitive nature. This is precisely what *Conversations with God* did as well.

There may be ideas that seem inconceivable, but I would heed the message given to me in the interview about making sure to go within before questioning something. "Misinterpretation is a plague of many, many centuries and many, many, many men." This is why I implore anyone who reads this to read it over and over again, and whenever you are unsure or stuck, simply ask, "Dear God, is this the accurate interpretation?" Then wait for an answer.

As bizarre as it is explaining to my friends and family how I interviewed "God" (a name I always hated) and as scary as it is to share this with strangers, there is beauty or perhaps karma in this irony. I feel compelled to share this book in the hopes that others may benefit from its teachings. You may not understand it, and you may not believe in some of these concepts. But your willingness to read or listen says you are open to a shift in consciousness.

I want to live in a better, more peaceful world, and I believe there is a way to do that by opening up to the truths of the Universe. Whether you are someone who is new to spiritual principles or someone who already understands them, this book will show you how we are all part of *The All of Everything*.

1 From Channel Changer to Spiritual Channel

I can't remember a time in my life when I didn't question everything in our world. Perhaps this desperate search for answers to life's grandest secrets is why I was drawn to journalism in the first place.

With laser-focused determination, I was able to become a correspondent for the *Access Hollywood* website and weekend show and make regular appearances on CNN, MSNBC, *Chelsea Lately*, and international programs as a pop culture expert. I even had the chance to play a fictional version of myself for the TV shows *Drop Dead Diva*, *Days of our Lives*, *General Hospital*, and *The Young and the Restless*. Smartly, I didn't go into a full-time career as an actress. I was terrible at it.

While I was living out my childhood dream of being an entertainment reporter on national television shows, as I got further and further into my career I longed for something more meaningful in my life, something much less superficial than all the Hollywood celebrity pomp and circumstance I was surrounded by. I was desperate to make the world better somehow and to get the answers to the mysteries of our universe.

What is life all about? Why do so many terrible things happen? Why can't humans be kind and take care of one another? Where did we all come from? Is there really a God? Oh, and why are we so obsessed with the Kardashians? You know, the really big, important stuff.

Throughout my life, nothing taught by religious institutions ever connected or clicked for me, but I also didn't consider myself to be an agnostic or an atheist. My beliefs fell somewhere between thinking there must be a powerful source we all come from but not believing in the type of God others worshipped as our judge, jury, and savior. I felt caught between two worlds.

Sometime in my twenties, bizarre things started happening to me. I began sensing energy or spirits. I felt a connection with what I believed at the time were spirits communicating with me from beyond the grave. I didn't have a clue as to where we go when we die, but I knew for sure something existed after death.

Being on national television didn't exactly make me want to shout out, "Hey, I think I talk to dead people!" So I kept my intuitiveness to myself and a few close friends and family members. I also sought psychics and mediums to further confirm my suspicions. I was shocked when one told me I too was psychic and "a channel." At that time, the only channels I knew about were the ones on my television.

It was after the deaths of my brother and my dad, with my life in shambles, that I was guided toward those who could help unravel those giant universal unknowns for me. Do our souls truly exist after we leave the earthly world? Is there something else?

I looked for those answers for two solid years first through a spiritual counselor, then through spiritual self-help books, such as those by Deepak Chopra, Wayne Dyer, and Marianne Williamson, audio downloads and classes, and finally through my own inner wisdom and guidance system (a.k.a. the voice within). The concepts not only resonated with me but also explained my intuitiveness. I was becoming a true believer in the concept of us being guided by a universal presence, which most would term God.

My life started to make sense. My two worlds were finally colliding. I was now *awake*, and the more I studied spiritual principles and trusted my own intuition, the more I started seeing signs and messages. The proof was all around me. We don't just die, and that's it. We are not alone in this great big universe. We do, in fact, have a source from where we all come—an energy system many term God. That energy seeks only to give and share unconditional love and to help us grow and evolve our souls; that energy is also inside of us.

Nowadays, more and more people are beginning to understand our connection to the universe thanks to yoga, mindfulness, meditation, and the spiritual celebrity poster girl, Oprah Winfrey. Mind-body-soul. It's not just trendy. It's truth.

Yet I still had questions. If God is always listening and answering our prayers to help us grow and evolve, then why is life so hard? Why do we worship celebrities? Why did my brother get cancer? What made my dad take his own life? How can we survive loss, death, and depression? Is there a better way to heal our hurts and make our world peaceful at last? Because if there were, I wanted to teach it, preach it, and shout it from the rooftops to anyone willing to listen.

Before I could do that, I needed answers, my own answers rather than words written by others. Spiritual studies had taught me to "go within" and listen to that quiet voice inside of me and when I finally did, an entirely new world opened up for me.

The thing is that the Universe (or Source or God) is always there to guide us. You just don't realize it because life can be difficult, frustrating, and hard, and the more stressful stuff you go through, the harder it can be to hear that quiet voice within. This is why those who do pray are sometimes not convinced that God is lending an ear or a helping hand. They feel lost and sure they are alone; they are too caught up in fears, doubts, and worries to notice the signs and messages we always receive. An inspired thought, a song on the radio reminding you of a lost loved one, a message of hope in your favorite movie or TV show or an overheard conversation between two friends or strangers. Those are for you.

These days, I know when a message is for me. I feel it in my gut. My instincts kick in instantaneously. I am always open and ready to receive guidance, and most importantly, I am always asking for it through prayer and intention (a sort of spiritual goal setting).

Talking to God (or Source or Spirit) and getting those inspired thoughts, signs, and messages takes work. Just like when you build body muscles, you have to be consistent in your practice to build spiritual muscles. Belief is the most powerful tool in your arsenal (your spiritual tool box), but to harness belief, we must be persistent and consistent in asking for help; we must remind ourselves we come from and are unconditional love.

As an entertainment reporter, I have interviewed some exceptionally famous people in my career. Beyonce, Halle Berry, Johnny Depp, Tom Hanks, and Selena Gomez come to mind. But nothing compares to asking the creator of the universe any and all questions that pop into your brain (even the gossipy ones). Leave it to a reporter to go after the scoop. Does God watch Netflix? Are celebrities like Jennifer Lopez chosen to be famous? Should we stop getting all this plastic surgery?

I'm pretty sure that Spirit inspired the questions in this book and placed them in my mind by putting me into situations that caused me to ask them. I wish I had the knowledge and ability on my own to write the way my mind (and hands) were guided to during this interview process. I am creative for sure, but writing this has been like an out-of-body experience, or at least an out-of-my-mind one!

Yet I tell you I am not out of my mind. I have seen, heard,

and experienced the living proof of what is possible when we stop trying to do everything ourselves and begin to cocreate with the Universe. I promise you that if you open your mind and pay attention to what is going on around you, your life can and will be forever changed.

2 Life Happens, and It Can Sometimes Really Suck.

To get to where I am now spiritually, a transformation had to occur. It's often when we are at our lowest point that we finally begin to seek the light. That's what I did subconsciously after a series of terrible events that took place in my life.

In the fall of 2010, my career was flourishing. I was working for *Access Hollywood* on camera after a decade as a producer. I had just been asked to cohost the first Emmys red-carpet live stream for NBC. It was a dream come true. I had also just met a seemingly great guy. My family was happy and healthy. Life was good. Yet, like in any good Hollywood story when things are going well, it all came crashing down.

Within a span of six years, I had gotten pregnant and was subsequently left for another woman by my son's biological father. My brother died of cancer. My dad committed suicide. On the bright side, I did marry a wonderful man. However, we lost two babies to miscarriage and suffered through three failed adoption attempts. I left my lucrative television job and was struggling career wise. To top it off, I ended up getting divorced and was diagnosed with skin cancer.

The downward spiral started a week after those 2010 Emmys. After five months of dating my boyfriend, I decided we should break up because we were in a long-distance relationship, and it was getting too hard to see each other. Five days after we broke up, I found out I was pregnant. I will never forget the day I had to tell my dad that his thirty-eight-year-old daughter was knocked up.

I found myself pregnant and alone. I struggled through a miserable pregnancy. I was constantly in pain emotionally and physically, and I cried all the time. And thanks to raging hormones, I contemplated suicide during an exceptionally tough moment.

My ex-boyfriend came in and out of my life while I was pregnant, and we wound up getting back together right before my son was born. Two months into my maternity leave, we were spending time together as a family. However, through what I am now certain was divine intervention, I found out he had been cheating on me with a multitude of women in numerous cities the whole of our relationship.

I confronted him, and things got very ugly. We ended up being the main story on various internet sites after a regretful confrontation with the TV matchmaker who had played a hand in setting us up. My boyfriend ultimately chose not to be a part of my son's life. My son was seven months old then, and as of the time this book was written, he has not seen his biological father since.

The longer I worked in Hollywood, the more I started to grow weary of the red-carpet world. I was so tired of dealing with celebrities and their holier-than-thou attitudes. And those attitudes were perpetuated by their "people" (a.k.a. publicists, managers, agents, and assistants) building them up and making those of us in the press feel like purveyors of trash.

My aggravation got the best of me backstage at *American Idol* one night, so I wrote an article calling out a certain female rapper and judge on her behavior. It did not go over well with her loyal fans, and they attacked. I tried to keep my dignity, but my ego was bruised, and I think my soul had dealt with enough entertainment news.

Six months later in November of 2013, my older brother Jason (forty-six years old at the time) was diagnosed with a terminal stomach cancer known as adenocarcinoma. The day he called to tell me the news, I collapsed on the floor in a sobbing fit of convulsions. Our family's world was shattered.

Jason was given just a few months to live. He started chemo and radiation therapy right away and survived for twelve months.

During that year, Jason and I spent a lot of time together. I traveled from Los Angeles to Vermont to see him as often as I could. Watching him slowly die before my eyes was heart-wrenching. I felt helpless. Despite how vastly different our lives were, we shared an amazing bond. Jason was an environmental scientist working toward saving our planet from climate change and the like; I was a Hollywood chick reporting on stories of drama, divorce, and drugs. He used to jokingly call me "the talent" and was always there to call me out if I ever copped a diva-like attitude. His death destroyed me. I retreated from the world, my friends, and my career. Already frustrated from the *American Idol* debacle, I quit my job at *Access Hollywood* four months after Jason passed.

My father, Stuart, struggled with depression after he retired from his job as a lawyer. He had a difficult childhood, an angry father who largely ignored him in favor of work and friends, and a mother who dealt with mental illness. Grandma Syd had even spent time in a mental hospital where she underwent brutal shock treatments as part of her therapy. I believe my dad felt mental illness would be a destiny he could not escape.

While I was pregnant with my son, my dad had shoulder surgery. He refused to take any pain medication. He fell into a deep depression during his recovery and landed himself in a mental hospital for a week. Fortunately, with the help of my mom, my brothers, and my dad's doctors, we were able to pull him out of what was deemed an anxiety disorder.

I think that after Jason, my dad's first born, was diagnosed with cancer and subsequently passed away, my dad lost his will to live. A recent diagnosis of COPD didn't help either. The depression returned, and unbeknownst to us, he stopped taking his anxiety medications. He slipped back into the anxiety disorder and wound up taking his own life sixteen months after my brother's death. After an initial attempt at cutting himself with a kitchen knife, he drowned himself in the lake by my house in Los Angeles. My dad was my rock, my cheerleader, and my biggest fan. He was my closest confidant. I was his pride and joy.

During this dark period of my life, I was blessed to have gotten married to a great guy. He helped me through these losses, but our relationship came with its own set of complications. His first wife had died of the same cancer as my brother's, and I felt guilt and shame for bringing death back into his and his daughter's lives so soon after his first wife, his daughter's mother, had passed.

Blending our families was also a challenge (as most couples who undertake this will admit), and though we planned to have a child together, we struggled with infertility.

Trying on our own didn't work, so after eight months of no pregnancy, we went to see an infertility specialist. Our first attempt with a procedure called IUI worked, and we were elated. But in my first trimester, while taking in a John Mayer concert at the Hollywood Bowl, I started feeling sick and had to run to the bathroom. Blood was everywhere, and we wound up losing the baby that night. Two months later, we found ourselves pregnant again only to lose that baby shortly after as well.

After those two miscarriages, doctors discovered I had a folic acid deficiency, which was causing the problems with staying pregnant. The fix for it was easy: take a baby aspirin and extra folic acid during pregnancy.

Unfortunately, we were never able to conceive again. So we decided to give domestic adoption a try. This presented its own set of challenges for which we were not emotionally prepared. Adoption is highly misrepresented in our society, and the risks and costs were far greater than we knew.

Within about seven months, we were matched with a birth mother who was having a baby girl. She was a woman in Texas who we later found out was scamming multiple families for money. We immediately received the shocking news when our adoption agency discovered the deceit. My dad had just died two days earlier, making this even more traumatic.

Four months after that, we matched with a birth mother in New York. Things were going well with her, except every time I spoke with her on the phone, she kept changing her story. It turned out she had been lying about who the father of her baby (and her other children) was because he was in the country illegally. We made the choice to walk away.

Our third adoption match would be our last and the most emotionally crippling. The couple we were matched with had already placed another child with a family in the past. In most adoption cases, this is a sign that a placement is a sure thing. The couple was also very young, had two other children they were raising, and had only one steady job between them. Red flags came up along the way but nothing that made us think this wasn't our baby. We were excited. The kids were excited. The grandparents were excited; my mom was especially looking forward to another grandchild to dote on after the loss of her son and husband.

For three months, we prepared for the baby to arrive. Friends gave us clothes and a car seat. We readied my son's old baby things. The day the baby (a girl) was born, our bags were packed and we were ready to head to the airport. However, we got the phone call you dread as a hopeful adoptive parent. The birth parents were thinking of changing their minds. They had been hiding the pregnancy from their parents and waited too long to go to the hospital. The baby was born at home, and the family (who lived close by) saw the ambulance and found out the secret. For two long days, we held our breath as the birth parents mulled over their choices.

Hope turned to devastation yet again.

It's hard to be angry at a couple who wanted to keep their own child, but the loss wrecked us emotionally. Financially, it was a huge loss as well. We had spent around $30,000 on the failed adoptions and the medical bills we racked up trying to conceive a child. The disrupted adoption (the term they use when the birth mom decides not to place the baby) was the final blow to our marriage. We tried to sort it out in marriage counseling, but ultimately, our sessions revealed hidden resentments, fears, and a refusal to compromise with each other. Our marriage imploded amid the anger, pain, and sadness.

Five babies lost, my dad and brother gone, my career in crisis, my marriage over. Had it not been for the spiritual journey I embarked on to help with the healing, I think I may have joined my father in that lake.

3
The Awakening Begins

Two months after my dad died, I was in the absolute darkest place I had ever been. Pajamas or Lululemons were my uniform for moping around the house. Looming over my head was a ConnectHer Media women's conference I had committed to attending. Under much duress, I made the three-hour drive to San Diego to get there. My soul was clearly in charge of that day's destination. It was where my spiritual journey began and what saved my life.

I had been invited as the writer of a new blog I had started called *Dish Detox*. It was a holistic health blog I created to honor my brother's memory. This became my passion project after leaving my job at *Access Hollywood*. The conference seemed like a good way to introduce myself to other bloggers and influencers. I had no idea at the time how it would wind up affecting me and my life's true purpose.

The founder of the conference shared the story of surviving a brain tumor. Another speaker had miraculously overcome stage III thyroid cancer and used it as fuel to start her now-thriving organic beauty business. Hope and a spark of optimism ignited. If these women could come back from death's door, I could come back from my traumas too.

Next, a marketing and branding expert spoke using spiritual principles to describe how "the Universe" could be our guide in our career goals. Her words intrigued me, and I wanted to know more. So I stalked her after the speech and revealed my sob story. Rather than feeling sorry for me, she implored me to check out the Center for Spiritual Living in Los Angeles. This was the place that had guided her on her path to enlightenment long ago.

The center turned out to be right near my house, so I had no excuse not to go. The night I arrived for a service, I headed straight for the bathroom (as I often do because I have the bladder of a ninety-year-old grandmother). While I was washing my hands, a stunning blond woman (a dead ringer for Heather Locklear) very earnestly grabbed my hand and said, "Hi, how are you? Welcome," with the biggest smile on her face. It felt as if an angel had crossed my path, and I instantly felt better about coming to this unfamiliar place.

The venue was set up like a church but in an office building. I sat down on a pew wondering what I had gotten myself into. "Is this a cult?" I asked myself. However, when I listened to the reverend explain how here they honor all paths to God, I realized I was in a nonchurch church. It didn't matter which path you choose, be it God, Universe, Source, Spirit, or something else, she said. It only mattered that you choose to believe in a power beyond yourself. I could get behind that, I thought.

As it turned out, the peppy lady in the bathroom was the evening's main speaker, Kim Stanwood Terranova. She was a spiritual life coach, and her presence on stage was magical. I hung on her every word.

"Are you present in your life? Are you laughing? Are you joyful? Are you grateful for the blessings you do have even when you have nothing, literally nothing, to be grateful for?" she inquired of the audience.

Nope. I certainly was not grateful at that moment. My life was a wreck, and I felt like a zombie existing only for my son. I sat in silence with tears in my eyes.

After I left, I made an appointment with Kim for one-on-one grief counseling. She worked out of her home, a stunning retreat in Malibu overlooking the mountains and ocean. The first time I sat in Kim's chair in her very Zen office, she stated, "I'm going to pray you in."

Prayer before a therapy session? This was a first for me.

She clasped her hands together, and we closed our eyes; I think I may have rolled my shut eyes at her wondering what good this would do me. Prayer was not my thing then.

As we spoke about my losses, her words resonated with me. She spoke not of spiritual principles in our first session but rather of human truths. "Grieving is a process." "There is no shame in hanging our head for a time after a loss." "Don't judge where you are in the process."

She also introduced me to some concepts that I had not heard of until I stepped into the Center for Spiritual Living about how we are guided by a force we cannot see, which she deemed "Spirit."

Other than prayer, God was left out of our first sessions, and for this I was glad. God was not someone I was too happy with at that moment. Growing up, I had never really prayed or thought of God. I had just kind of believed a higher power existed (though not as some dude in a white gown sitting on a throne holding a bo staff). But when you take away my dad and brother and babies, yep, I blamed God for all these tragedies. I was not ready to hear from nor pray to a God who would do such things. And what about 9/11 or all these mass shootings in America, I thought. What sort of God would do that? Nope. Keep God out of my life.

In fact, even as I went further into my sessions with Kim, I was still wary of the word "God" and much preferred her terminology of Source, Universe, and Spirit. Many times, she would stop talking and consult with Spirit by listening to the words she was hearing in her head. Usually the most eloquent or thought-provoking explanation of my current anguish or problem would come out of her mouth.

When I complained that nothing in my life was working or changing, Kim let me vent but would always drive the conversation back to one specific question: "What is your daily practice?"

At first, I had none. I would lie and tell her I did, but in truth I might have read a book passage in some spiritual book or written out a few things I was grateful for in a journal; but I never prayed, and I certainly never meditated. Trying to quiet my mind was as easy as getting a bull to step gingerly through a china shop.

As our sessions went on, Kim introduced me to intention and offered recommendations on spiritual books to read. I became very intrigued by *The Law of Attraction* in which a woman named Esther Hicks channels a group of beings who speak through her and call themselves Abraham.

I bought CDs, downloaded audio books, and even got my first library card since college. Deepak Chopra, Wayne Dyer, Gabrielle Bernstein, Marianne Williamson—if they wrote it, I read it or listened to it.

I felt I had some type of intuitive gift, and I needed to learn more. I also joined mediumship seminars and took classes on clairvoyance.

Once I began to take these classes, strange incidents of connecting with Spirit began to happen more frequently. One night in my clairvoyance class, I felt as if I was choking and could not breathe. I heard the name Emily in my head. I made the teacher stop the class because I was so frantic. She cleared the energy from the room and asked any spirits wanting to communicate to leave. I instantly felt better and we continued with the class. At the end, before everyone left, I asked my classmates if anyone had known an Emily who had died. The girl sitting right next to me was stunned. She had lost a friend named Emily to suicide by hanging.

Later, in one of Kim's seminars, "Here's Johnny"[2] (in that creepy Jack-Nicholson-from-*The-Shining* way) repeated in my head. I couldn't shake the feeling that this had something to do with someone in the room. It turned out, as I learned later that day, Kim's very dear friend had lost her son just two weeks prior. His name? Johnny.

Once during a massage, I kept hearing the word "Peebles" and asked the therapist if she knew anyone with that name. She did not. Two weeks later at a mediumship class, a student in the class excitedly introduced himself to me. He knew I worked in television. He was writing a movie about a doctor who had died a hundred years ago and could be channeled through psychic mediums. The guy asked me if I would read his manuscript. It was a film about a man named Dr. Peebles, he explained. My eyes widened and my mouth fell open.

I knew I needed to "meet" this Peebles character. I was pretty sure the old dude wanted to talk to me. I had a session with a medium in California who channeled the good dead doctor. The whole thing was bizarre, but Dr. Peebles did seem to know a lot about my life and even some past lives. I recall the woman who was doing the channeling telling me I too was a channel. She was very adamant that she give me the name of someone who could help me open up my channel so I too could communicate with Spirit. I took the information but never did anything with it because I frankly found the whole notion of channeling very strange. It turns out she was right though. I am a channel. I can channel "God."

The more of a believer I became in Spirit, signs, and messages, the more they showed up. I was having a reading with a celebrity palm reader at a Golden Globes gift lounge. She connected me to my brother and told me things about him she could not have known without channeling him.

"Oh, he is a funny one," she laughed. "He plans to play lots of jokes on you."

As I left the building, I got on the elevator alone, and the doors kept opening and closing. I knew it was my brother.

I started noticing how the radio would play certain songs with very specific titles or messages just when I needed them, usually in a series of three. Animals, which I learned carry special messages for us, started showing up in random places. Grasshoppers, doves, snakes, mice, rats, raccoons, rabbits. A book on animal spirit guide symbolism helped me decipher the messages.

I also began noticing license plates with little sayings that seemed to relate directly to me and what was going on in my life. OBLADI1 zoomed past me one morning on the freeway while I was thinking about and missing my dad. The next morning on that same stretch of road, a different car whizzed by; OBLADA its license plate read. *"Ob-la-di, Ob-la-da."* Life really does go on! My dad was letting me know he was in fact hanging around me.

My depression began to lift, and I was enjoying the consistent songs and license plate messages. Dragonflies and butterflies seemed to follow me around reminding me always of my dad and brother.

I received another book recommendation, *A Course in Miracles.*[3] I needed a miracle in my life I thought, but when I started reading it, the book's terminology was very Christian in nature and referenced God and Jesus. Not being religious, I felt this was not my cup of tea. So after I bought the book and tried reading it, I wound up returning it to the store. Yet a nagging feeling that I was meant to read that book would not go away. So I rebought it a couple months later and dove in.

The concepts were completely foreign to me. It presented the quite-simple-in-nature notion that every thought comes from either Love or Fear and inside each of us is an internal teacher (the Holy Spirit or Jesus) who is with us always. Whenever we take to prayer (the holy instant) and commune with the Holy

Spirit (Jesus), we have this helper alongside us to guide us back to love (salvation); and thus, a miracle occurs.

I decided to give the principles in *A Course in Miracles* a shot. What did I have to lose? I began to say little prayers even though at this point I was not a believer in the power of prayers. I also set intentions for myself as Kim, the spiritual counselor, had taught me to do.

"My intention is to sell my house," I wrote.

"Dear God, please help me through this divorce," I prayed repeatedly.

As I waited for these miracles to occur, they didn't seem to be happening. I got mad, frustrated, sad, and worried. My house wasn't selling. My career was stalled. I had virtually no money to live on. But I remembered what Kim had told me: "When we are in the midst of life's worst challenges is when we must pray the hardest."

Despite seeing no evidence of anything changing in my life, I kept praying, setting those intentions, and tossing in a little gratitude for good measure. As I did that, those license plates showed up all the time. The butterflies and dragonflies continued to follow me around as if to say, "Keep going!"

The day that shifted my perspective on whether or not prayer and intention actually worked was the day before I had Mohs surgery for a basal cell skin cancer on my face. My good friend Kristy, a makeup artist I worked with in my twenties, died at age thirty-six of melanoma, and this was weighing heavily on my mind.

I was reminded of a quotation in *A Course in Miracles*[4] with a striking message. "If the mind can heal the body, but the body cannot heal the mind, then the mind must be stronger than the body," the book said.

Could I really heal my body through prayer? Had I created this for myself? The day before my skin cancer surgery, I was in complete panic mode. I put all the spiritual principles I had been learning into my arsenal, including some energy healing techniques taught to me in my clairvoyance class. During my drive to work, I prayed for help to calm my fears about the upcoming procedure.

"Please help alleviate my fears about this skin cancer; show me only love is real. Amen," I pleaded.

For some reason, I decided to stop at a Rite Aid near my office. I usually never ran errands before work. Pulling into a parking space, I glanced at the car next to mine; the black SUV had a license plate, which read FEELOVE. Feel Love. As I pulled out of the parking lot, a dragonfly flew right by my windshield. It was a sure sign and a message for me.

Ten hours later on my drive home from work, I was back in panic mode about the surgery. My boss had freaked me out by telling me the spot on my face didn't "look good."

Yet again, I prayed for help to calm my fears about the surgery. "Dear God, please show me that everything is going to be OK tomorrow, and remove this fear."

All of a sudden, that same black SUV with the FEELOVE license plate pulled in front of my car. What were the odds that at the exact moment of prayer, the exact same car would find its way to me in a city of twelve million people? Spiritual teachers will tell you there are no coincidences. Until that moment, I would have never truly believed it.

I would love to tell you that from this moment on I was a spiritual gangster who walked the spiritual walk with birds singing and rainbows shooting from my ears. I wasn't. At this point, I believed more and more in (and certainly saw more proof of) our connection to the Universe, but I still wasn't 100 percent onboard.

At the very least, I would turn to my spiritual tools more often. Intention, prayer, meditation, gratitude—some days they helped put me in a better mood and other days not so much. On one especially horrible day while I was going through my divorce, I wrote this prayer in one of my journals.

Dear God, these last six years have been so incredibly hard in terms of loss. Loss of my brother, my dad, five babies, and now my husband. I am ready to move to a higher vibration and manifest a different experience now. One of abundance, joy, love, and more children. I'm asking for guidance that will take me quickly to my next chapter and show me what my divine purpose in life is. I no longer wish to be lost. I wish to be guided by Spirit. I surrender my heart to you. I surrender to the Universe that LOVE is the only thing, and every day I will continue to see only LOVE until I have everything I want and need.

Did things change instantaneously? Absolutely not. I still felt pain and hardships, and I fell back into fear, doubt, and worry. But I stuck to those spiritual tools and continued to pray every day and use intentions.

"Dear God, please take away my fears and doubts and worries as I move toward abundance, joy, and love," I would say repeatedly.

Some days were good; others were more challenging. Frustrations and setbacks occurred, but as I continued to stay in daily practice as Kim had asked me to do during our first months together, my life started to change.

I was no longer angry. I was able to forgive pretty much everyone who I felt had done terrible things to me: the man I blamed for derailing my on-camera career in Hollywood, the girl who stole my spotlight, the internet haters for attacking me, the man who chose to love another instead of me and walk away from his child, and my dad and brother for dying. I left bitterness and resentment behind for the first time in my life. It felt good. I felt lighter and freer.

I decided I also needed a fresh start away from the chaos of Hollywood and the entertainment industry. The whole time

I prayed for and set intentions to find the perfect house in the perfect neighborhood, friends, and the right school to send my son to.

We moved to Florida, to be near my brother Mike and his two kids and amazing serendipities were everywhere. The couple who sold me our house ended up being long-time friends of my neighbor and mommy friend in Los Angeles. The wife from the couple introduced me to a fantastic group of ladies in the neighborhood. One girl from the group had gone to my high school in Pennsylvania and another turned out to be an old friend of my dear friend in Florida. The Universe was working on my behalf for sure.

I had new friends and a beautiful new home. My son loved his new school and his new friends. I was living closer to my niece and nephew. I had a fantastic job, which landed in my lap and allowed me to work from home. These were all things I had prayed about and had set an intention for. I finally stopped focusing on the terrible things that happened in my life and started feeling unburdened. I was confident that we actually do have spiritual helpers. That's when the voice within started speaking to me.

4

Death Becomes Her

To quote my late father, "Let me give you some history here." (After saying this, he would then tell the world's longest story about something.)

I think my journey to spirituality began when I was about eight years old. I thought a lot about death even though at the time I didn't know anyone who had died.

A few days before my eleventh birthday, my nana, my mom's mom, passed away. I remember lying in my bed surrounded by my stuffed animals for comfort and thinking about what it would be like when I was not here anymore. A frightening sensation reverberated through my body.

Over the years, I have talked to many friends and family members who have mentioned they know exactly that feeling. The pit in your stomach, the dread that overcomes you as you think how strange it will be when you are dead and gone. If you are still someone who gets that doomed sense when you think about death, this book will be a big help for you. By the time you are done reading it, you will know that fearing death is as silly as fearing a lion suddenly showing up at your doorstep to eat you.

In my early teens, I went from fearing death to pondering

where we go when we die. My grandfather and a friend of mine from high school had also passed away at this point. I quizzed my parents,

"What happens when you die?"

"When you're dead, you're dead. There is nothing else. You go in the ground," my mom told me.

This concept made no sense to me. Lights out, game over? No way. I don't know how, but I knew she was wrong.

At my grandmother Syd's funeral, when I was older, I refused to participate in the custom of throwing dirt on the coffin. I felt it was rude and that she would see me and not appreciate it.

In my twenties, I began to sense energy in houses and buildings. "Somebody died here," I would proclaim as the hairs stood up on my arm. I was proven right 90 percent of the time by friends or family members who knew the history of the homes. They all were baffled by how I could know this. So was I.

In my thirties, I began hearing words and thoughts in my head as well as sensing those "ghosts." I had just moved into my first home in California, and within about a week, I heard what sounded like the voices of a man and woman talking to each other in the middle of the night. The voices sounded as if they came from inside the floorboards of my bedroom. For two nights, they conversed while I searched everywhere inside and outside to figure out where the voices were truly coming from. No explanation presented itself. Fortunately, the voices stopped and never returned. I enlisted the help of my neighbor Marlene to solve the mystery.

"Has anyone ever died in my house?" I asked her the next morning.

Marlene's eyes widened, and her face turned white. Decades earlier, her son had been mowing the lawn across the street when the man who had owned my home at that time collapsed in the driveway from a heart attack. He literally died in her son's arms. I felt terrible making her relive this awful memory, but I had to know more.

"So what happened to his wife?" I inquired.

The wife was living in a nursing home in northern California, she explained. Marlene wrote the name and number for the nursing home down on a slip of paper. I took it to work, and with my hands shaking, I dialed the number. I'm pretty sure my soul already knew what I was about to hear.

"Oh, I'm very sorry miss. She died two days ago," an employee at the nursing home revealed.

Goosebumps ran up my arms, and I remember jumping up from my desk and screaming, "Oh my god!" I freaked out my coworkers as I explained the voices and how two days ago they had disappeared. Later, a psychic medium blessed the house and explained how when the wife crossed over, she met up with her true love in the place where she had last seen him. Lovers reunited. I get goosebumps now even writing this.

I was even able to sense my brother on the evening after he passed away. My parents and I were picking up my other brother, Mike, at the airport, and despite our grief, we decided to go get something to eat. I remember walking toward a pizza parlor and smelling curry, a very strong odorous version of it. It didn't make sense why a pizza place would smell that way. I looked around to see if perhaps an Indian restaurant was nearby, but there wasn't one. Inside the pizza place smelled as it should, like pizza. I knew this curry-ous odor was a sign from my departed brother. Jason and I had a long-running joke about curry. He loved it, and I absolutely despised the pungent smell and flavor, deeming it "vile curry." This would be the first of many Jason signs and messages to come.

Though I still was skeptical of my strange intuitive abilities, words began popping into my head at random. I had lunch with a friend one afternoon. Her cousin had recently committed suicide, and my friend thought we could console each other. I kept hearing the words "white purse" in my head as we chatted.

When I mentioned this to my friend, she explained that she was the one who had to clean out her cousin's apartment, and the only item she kept of her cousin's belongings was a white purse.

Even on the day my dad died, my Spidey senses were tingling. I recall standing in our guest room (where my dad had slept on occasion). My mom called to tell me my dad had taken the car and had gone missing. I stood there with goosebumps and already knew that my dad was dead. I kept hearing the word "ducks" in my head, so I grabbed the keys and drove frantically to the pond where I used to take my son to feed the ducks. I was heartbroken when I did not find my dad or the car. Later on, it turned out the ducks I kept thinking about were the ones in a lake that was by my house. I am pretty sure dad was trying to guide me to the place where I could find him, but we got our wires crossed.

When I told her the concept of this book (and boy, was I terrified to tell her about it), my very less-than-open-minded mom was actually not shocked at all. She had seen some of my signs and messages and had even been a participant in some of them. About a year ago, my mom lost her pocket address book. She kept everything in that book, and she was frantic. We drove all over town going back to places where she could have dropped it. I kept saying I felt that it was in the parking lot next to the Jamba Juice where we had been an hour prior. We spent another hour driving around looking for it, but we came up empty handed. Sure enough, when we finally drove back to Jamba Juice, not only was the address book sitting on the ground where we had parked the car, but it also seemed as if no one had even parked in that spot while we were gone. The address book was untouched, which was odd for such a busy shopping center. Mom got back in the car and closed the door. I turned to her and said, "You watch. I bet we are going to see a dragonfly right now." (My symbol for when my dad and brother were hanging around.) Right as I said it, a gigantic, orange dragonfly flew by the windshield. My mom was stunned.

5 Soul Searching

Before we get to the interview, it may help to understand what spiritual principles I was familiar with when I started asking the questions of God. To ask the right questions, I now see I needed to have some understanding, some knowledge (or now I would say, remembering) of a grander vision of life.

- Your thoughts and emotions are what create your life. This is the concept written about in the best-selling books *The Secret*[5] and *The Law of Attraction*[6].
- God will never violate our free will. We are free to think whatever thoughts we want and have whatever emotions we want. However, we attract to ourselves situations and experiences based on those thoughts and emotions and our actions.
- Our souls are the essence of who we are, and our intuition is our souls guiding us. Our egos are the parts of our minds that view us as being separate from the energy system from which we all emanate.
- We each have an internal teacher who guides us back to love (salvation) and who we can turn to in prayer at

any time. *A Course in Miracles*[7] would call this the Holy Spirit or Christ. You will see I prayed throughout my talk with God to make sure we got the words correct and nothing made it into the book that should not be here.

- Only two emotions exist: love and fear. Love is real. Fear is an illusion, meaning that anything that comes from fear is actually not really happening to us. We just think it is. I understood this concept best after reading Marianne Williamson's best-selling book *A Return to Love* which received worldwide attention after Williamson appeared on *The Oprah Winfrey Show* decades ago. Oh, and a little movie franchise called *Star Wars* is based on this concept of love versus fear.
- We are all one and a part of God (or Universe or Source). The only difference between us and God is that God created us, but we did not create God. Wayne Dyer spoke in his seminars of this as God being the ocean and us being the waves. I like to say God is the cake and we are the slices.
- We are eternal beings, only our bodies die. Our souls live on. We have always been and will always be.
- We are here to grow and evolve our souls, and this is why we have many lifetimes. We call it reincarnation. (You will learn later in the book why this term is inaccurate.)
- Gratitude, daily practice of prayer, intention (goals you set for yourself), and meditation are necessary to stay in a place of higher spiritual contact with our higher self, spiritual masters, and also angels and guides.
- Spirits can and do communicate with us from heaven (or wherever we go when we die) and can send us signs and messages. Most of the time we miss these because we are too caught up in our human drama.

- The mind creates all illnesses in the body. The late Louise Hay was a pioneer in the mind-body-soul connection (the book *You Can Heal Your Life* is a great resource on this). Medical scientists are starting to see a mind-body connection too.
- Time and space do not exist in the spirit world the same way they do on earth.

With all these ideas in my realm of knowledge, I went into writing my own book as a way to help others who are dealing with tragedy, trauma, or depression.

6 God—The Interview, Part One

"Dear God, please allow my words, our words, to flow out easily and effortlessly so we may share your message with the masses. Please remove anything in the material that does not serve our higher good. I accept this information as truth and am grateful for all we are meant to learn and remember. Amen."

God: Then we shall begin.

Laura: Where shall we begin?

G: Wherever you want.

L: Let's start with money because that seems to be the driving force of my fears. What are my blocks to abundance? Why do I have so much fear when it comes to money?

G: Fear is of the mind, not of the body. The only way to release fear is through the mind by giving it back to me. I do not wish for anyone to be without money, for it is how you get things in your universe. I only want that people learn the value of money, as it is a commodity that establishes the order of giving and getting. In order to get, you must give. In order to give, you must know that you have and are enough. In order to be enough, you must believe that all you are is all there is, and therefore, nothing can be taken from you. So when you give something away, you are just giving it back to yourself. The exchange is merely a handing off to yourself to and through another.

L: What is one thing I can do to bring abundance into my life?

G: You already have abundance. It is everyone's right to have it. I established it that way. You cannot, however, have abundance when every thought you think is of not having abundance. What do you not have? Nothing. So why would you think you don't have everything? You in fact have everything. It is sitting right next to you. You just cannot see it and, therefore, do not believe in its existence.

L: I do that. That is true.

G: Of course it is. It is spiritual law. That which you feel you are lacking is that which you are keeping away from yourself. Release the fear, and that which you already are will show up in your experience.

L: And what is it that we already are?

G: You already are everything. You are one with the Universe. You are cocreators, each and every one of you.

L: When I hear you, it sounds like a quiet voice inside of my head. I am not sure if it's my voice or a nonvoice. Why can others hear your voice externally, but I can only hear it internally?

G: My voice is created by what you believe. If someone believes they can hear me outside of them, then they will. The sound will still be coming from within, but they will believe, with their own ears, that I am talking to them externally. Truth will show it was always your voice. We are cocreators. You do not need me to answer. You know the answer within.

L: So am I talking to myself or talking to God?

G: Yes.

L: What do you mean, yes?

G: I am God. You are God. We are all God. I was just here before you came.

L: Are you more powerful than me?

G: No.

L: What happens if I turn away from God? Am I on my own?

G: Well, no. Of course you are not on your own. That is not possible at all. What is possible is you will decide for yourself, and many times deciding for yourself will bring you results you do not like. Therefore, it is always best to consult with your cocreator in every instant.

L: Where am I holding onto fear?

G: You are not holding onto fear so long as you are releasing it to me in every moment. The best way to ensure creation does not come into existence is to release the fear back to God and say, "This is a thought I no longer wish to have. I give it to God to remove from my subconscious mind."

L: And that is really all there is to it?

G: Indeed. It's so simple. Yet mathematically one cannot wrap their head around this concept. One plus one is two; sure that makes sense in the realm of the physical. In the realm of the unseen, one plus one equals everything. The All of Everything is all there is.

L: Why can we not get this? Why do we not understand we all come from the same source and are not separate beings?

G: Because you are beings, being separate. Being separate makes you feel as if all things are happening at random to you, not through you.

L: And that is why we can't get this?

G: Precisely.

L: Well, people want proof, and because there is no proof, then they say spirituality and universal truths are BS.

G: No proof? What of wars?

L: How would war be proof of a universal presence?

G: If God is all there is and is the All of Everything, would it not make sense that God is behind all wars?

L: Why on earth would God want us to go to war?

G: God does not want you to be at war. As the All of Everything, God wants peace, joy, love, and enlightenment for all. God is, however, part of everything. Therefore, we are all related in spiritual philosophy. We are all one giant being of light and love – Universal Energy through and through. There is no thing we are not.

L: Why, if we are just this Universal Energy system do we even use the term God throughout this book?

G: Why not? We will touch on this time and time again for the simple reason that it needs to be stated again and again, for those who wish to understand universal principles. We will use a word that is practical not preferable (a.k.a. God) to demonstrate a point we are trying to make here that all minds are responsible for the all of everything. So when one mind thinks, all minds think. We will speak of this later on as well. One mind sees a brother or sister and wishes to attack; another mind meets up with this thought and betrayal occurs.

L: And when more minds come together—

G: In anger and in venom, then the chaos of irrational thinking becomes like a choir of enemies and creates conditions where war becomes possible. God cannot stop this, as stopping it would violate one's free will thinking. It is, therefore, upon each individual mind to create the space where war is not a possibility.

L: That's a pretty bold concept. Although I still don't see how it's proof of a God or Universal Presence, especially considering some of the things that have happened to me.

G: Not to you, because of you. We will discuss this concept further on as well.

L: Then why did we lose the baby girl we were set to adopt on the day she was born? How am I the cause of that?

G: No. You are the effect of it. It was her free will. She was not yet ready to grow and evolve as she initially planned within the confines of your family dynamic. She made a choice as did you.

L: It was not my choice to lose her! At least not consciously. Was it perhaps my soul running the show?

G: Yes. Soul growth comes in many forms. Some circumstances your ego may have no control in. This is why, perhaps, it feels as if you are banging your head against a brick wall and there is no movement forward or you are moving backward, in a sense on some matters. Whenever soul and ego clash, a ripple effect is created and circumstances may be very jarring to the all of you.

L: So, my ego and soul clashed on this matter?

G: Yes, and subconsciously you knew this as well. Therefore, she was not yours to keep.

L: Don't soul and ego clash all the time?

G: Not necessarily. For we will cover this in depth later on. Instead let us ask what lesson would you say you have learned through that experience?

L: That fear is keeping me from having what it is I desire. I am so fearful of losing another child (among other things) that I have given up on the notion pretty much altogether.

G: Lose the fear, and the child, or children, will appear in your reality.

L: What about my dad and brother dying? Am I the cause of that?

G: Of course not. Your dad and brother dying are not part of your journey but rather theirs. It is their decisions that led to their demise on this plane. One need only look at the thoughts chosen by them to decipher and decode the reasons behind their "deaths" and what was the cause there. However, one cannot choose wrong, because wrong choice is a decision too. We cannot know what day our lives will end, but we can know what direction we will choose to go because we chose it purposefully.

L: I feel as if we are getting off track.

G: Only because you do not understand yet what I mean about death. You have heard that death is a continuing of life, but death is also just a continuing. So there really is no death.

L: So then where are they?

G: They are here. They are there. They are everywhere. You hold anger and bitterness and resentment. You are not mad at me or them but at yourself for not being where they are, but where they are actually is right here. You just can't see them with your physical eyes. They are in the trees, the grass, the leaves, the sunshine, the air. We are all around you, always. We see you, but you don't see us. That is by design, but it is not by design. It just is.

L: How can I better connect with them?

G: Feel their love in your heart, and then you will know them better.

L: What about the signs and messages I have seen from them?

G: Do you believe them?

L: Yes.

G: Then they are true for you.

L: How are mediums able to bring such incredible insightful readings to clients?

G: You can do exactly the same. You are a powerful medium as well, for I have made you that way. I have made you all that way. No one is more special than anyone else, but some feel the calling, and some don't. You feel the calling but are scared of what you might learn.

L: Why would I be scared of what I would learn?

G: Because it will unlock a part of you that you are not ready to unlock. A new door is opening, and you may step through it.

L: And what happens when I do step through it? Wow. I do feel the fear welling up in me right now.

G: Then you will unlock a grand identity, which will define where your life goes from here.

L: And where is that?

G: To be a teacher, a provider of healing.

L: I feel that, but I am also terrified of starting over. Lately it feels as if I am ready for a new chapter in my life but also as if I am going in slow motion and unsure of my next steps. What can I do about my career? Why does it feel as if I am stalled?

G: You are not stalled but rather delayed in your plan, which is my plan as well. You are a powerful communicator, yet you have been communicating to the wrong audience. I know who is ready, and you are also not ready yet. There will come a day when all that you know will come pouring out of you so easily and effortlessly that you will not have a need to communicate with me to gain the answers. You will help many people. It may not be the people you think, but it will be powerful.

L: If you say that I am the creator of my experience, but you have a plan for me, then doesn't that negate me being the creator?

G: We are cocreators. We decide together. Your soul knows what is best for you. Your inner voice wants to write the chapter (while your ego wants to write the book and be done with it), but you are the author of your book, and I am the publisher. We made the decision together that this is how it would go. You know deep down that this is the truth, but you refuse to believe that you can do such a thing, but let me tell you that you can, and you will.

L: What if I want to do something else?

G: Then you will because it is your free will, but don't you know that you know what is best for you and that I know what is best for you, and therefore, we should make the decision together in love? The you who is part of me knows that your purpose here on earth is to spread a message of love and peace and change. The you who has been hurt and angered and made to feel small believes you need to be seen to be heard. But there is a way to be heard that doesn't have to involve a part of society that does not want to hear it. There will be many more of those in your society than those who do want to hear it. You are capable of so much if only you can believe that.

L: What do I have to do to change my life for the better?

G: Nothing at all because I will do it for you.

L: But what does that mean?

G: It means in order to evolve and accept a new understanding of how life truly works, we must be cocreators. In your separation are you guided by ego's truths. In our loving arms are you found.

L: I'm sorry, but it just can't be that easy.

G: It is that easy but is not instantaneous. A life worth living is a life filled with highs and lows, ups and downs. There will be peaks and valleys. Wouldn't it be better to have more peaks than valleys? To do this, one must be consistent in the daily practice of commune with the All That Is (a.k.a. God).

L: Why is it so hard to let go of fear, doubt, and worry?

G: Because it is human nature, but it is not the common way to be in our universe. It is only where you are in the plane of existence.

L: Are there other places?

G: Yes. Many. You know this. You feel this. We all know this within.

L: Why have we not found them?

G: Because you are not ready.

L: Will we ever be ready?

G: Yes. There will come a time. That is all I can say on the matter for now. We will discuss this further in our next book. One must first understand universal principles here before expanding into other territories or concepts.

L: I know people are going to hear about this book and say

I am crazy. They will say that I am not talking to God but merely writing my own thoughts and feelings.

G: Do you think you are crazy?

L: No.

G: Then that is all that matters.

L: I know it's truth because I have seen the signs and messages for myself. I recognized the times where I created experiences in my life and drew people to me. I recognize the moments where I knew it was my dad and brother guiding me or helping me feel their presence. Where are they? Where is heaven?

G: Heaven is all around you. It is within you. It is you. Your loved ones are with you at all times, just not in the way you are used to or would like.

L: Can they see me?

G: Oh, yes. Not in a way that would make you uncomfortable, but from a place of love they can experience you. They know you better now than they did then because they can feel what you feel and can guide you from that place.

L: How do they guide you?

G: The same way I do, by thoughts, feelings, and messages.

L: Are they dead?

G: No. No one really dies, and no one really lives. They are spirits now just as you will be again.

L: Can they take forms of bodies again?

G: Yes, but only when they "reincarnate."

L: Why do we reincarnate?

G: To learn and grow and evolve.

L: Why do we leave our loved ones behind?

G: It is not leaving but a returning to who they really were, which is so much more than their bodies.

L: But as humans, death is so hard on us.

G: If you could only understand that death is just a change in circumstance, you would not be so sad all the time, but I do know that death in the human concept can be painful. Grief is necessary, I believe, for our evolvement. How can we know love unless we experience death? I know it is a hard concept to grasp, but it is not a concept that we take lightly, and that is why your loved ones are already around you the minute they "die," as you call it. You can experience them, just in a different way.

L: But it's so hard to not be able to see them or feel them with the physical body, especially parents who lose children.

G: This is a concept that I very much understand why it is so hard for you. Just know that nothing I do, we do, is without great consideration. They have chosen their path for a reason, which we cannot judge. We cannot hold onto the idea of pain when what we want to experience is joy. There is a way for a parent who has lost a child to experience that love of a child.

L: How does someone recover from that loss?

G: Know that they are with you always in a different way. Try to experience them that way as best as you can.

L: And how is that?

G: Live, love, and laugh, and they will live, love, and laugh with you. Do not overthink the death concept, as it cannot and will not change. You are here to experience joy, but you are in a body that is not here forever. Forever is a human concept that supersedes eternity, but in reality, eternity is not forever, as forever implies there is a beginning, and there is not.

L: So come to terms with the fact that we are not going to live forever?

G: Yes. In that body. As a spirit, you are eternal, as I am eternal.

L: What about signs and messages like I have been seeing? Do they actually exist?

G: A better question is do I send you signs and messages.

L: Yes. All the time.

G: In the rainbows. In the clouds. In a photograph. In a car. In a restaurant. In a conversation. In a dark alley. In a Popsicle.

L: Seriously? In a Popsicle?

G: Anywhere you are, I am. So, therefore, I am always sending you signs and messages. Pay attention, and the best road map you have ever had can guide you to the best place you will ever be.

L: How do you miss the signs and messages?

G: By using your own GPS and not downloading mine.

L: What is the highest vision for my life?

G: Being one with God and being a teacher.

L: Why do different teachers write different words and interpretations?

G: When you are writing from a space of cocreating with Spirit and the Universe or God (as most call it), you can never get it wrong. The words I am using are the words I know you recognize, but they are not words that every teacher uses. That is why it is best to ask and have answered the questions yourself. There is great value in other people's words but there is more value in your own. To sit quietly and know yourself, as I know you, is more valuable than any book, any movie, and any other's interpretation of my love. But what must be known is that the Bible and other great interpretations that have been dictated from man to man are not the whole truth. You know this. That is why you have come seeking me yourself. Your soul holds the truth for you, for it has always known and always will know. Your best option is to bet on yourself, bet on your words spoken to and with God. For only then can it be truth. Do not let the ego destroy your faith in what I am telling you. Do not let your ego run the show or write the script. Do not let the ego do anything that will harm your words. Words of harm are not of God. Only words of love are of God. The Bible will never be the right way to learn of God because it is not completely of God. Oh, there are passages and words that have made it into that book, and that is all it is, a book, but there are untruths about my vengeance. My will will never be vengeance against man; of mankind it will be only love. I cannot teach you anything but this, for it would be violating the rules of the universe, of which I am. I am the Universe.

L: What is your true name, then?

G: I Am.

L: But what does that mean?

G: It means I am as I am. There is nothing more for me to do or say on that subject. I am as I am. I have always been and always will be.

L: So we should call you "I Am" instead of God?

G: Yes, if you like. I only ask that you call or speak to me as I Am without interpretation.

L: I don't understand what you mean?

G: What I mean is that God is a term made by man to define something. The word has not meaning unless it has meaning to you. If it has meaning to you, then it is the perfect word to describe me. If the word inspires fear or anger or resentment, then it is not right for you. Only you know what is right for you. Your soul knows the truth.

L: We hear so much these days about meditation. I am terrible at it. How can we learn to meditate better?

G: So much has been made about meditation. This again is just another word that replaces quietness, stillness. Just sit down. Say nothing. Do nothing.

L: How do I turn off all those thoughts that come rushing in?

G: Turn them into questions. I will answer them, always.

L: What about visualization. Does that work, as many say it does?

G: If you believe it, then it will be true for you.

L: So it works, then?

G: Yes, if you believe it will.

L: What about sickness?

G: All sickness is of the mind, not the body. This is an incontrovertible fact. The body is a learning device for the mind. That is its only function on earth. When you learn through love, then your body will know love. When you learn through fear, then you will know pain and illness. In every moment, you are learning something, and your outer body reflects this. Sickness is not real as much as the body is not real.

L: How can we get unsick?

G: Unlearn what you have known all along that has been taught to you by your parents, your teachers, and your society. God is never sick. Therefore, you are never sick. Sickness is of the mind. It cannot be said enough.

L: Why does it take so long to heal when we are sick?

G: Does it take long? Time is irrelevant. Perhaps it is only your thought of it taking long that makes it seems long. It is in fact instantaneous, but only you can make manifest that ultimate healing reality.

L: When I am talking to you and asking questions and you are answering, I am hearing the words in my head. Will there be times when I write the wrong answer?

G: No. It is not possible.

L: What about the ego getting involved?

G: You will know when it is time to stop, as I will know when it is time stop. We are cocreators; therefore, no words can be written and kept that come from the ego. Do you fear that this will happen? If you do, then you must give those fears back to me by simply asking me to take them. This way there will be no question of what is truth and what is illusion.

L: It seems that before I even ask a question, you already have the answer for me.

G: This is true because it is true. I know what you want to ask of me before you know it. This is transformation in its highest form. We have come to a relationship where we may now cocreate.

L: What is the problem with my skin. I have psoriasis and it's been under control for a long time but now it's back with a vengeance.

G: There is no problem with your skin other than your belief system about yourself.

L: How can I change my skin problems and transform them?

G: Give them back to me for release. You suffer only because you believe you can suffer. When you are ready to view the truth, all of your so-called illnesses will thus then disappear.

I stopped writing and went to bed and the next day was out with my son. When we came home, there was a snake that slithered by me at the front door. I had read and believed that animals, when they appear to just us or in an unusual manner, are usually a message.

L: Tell me about the snake I just saw at my front door?

G: Transformation is at your front door. All you need do now is let it in, and we will move mountains together.

L: Not literal mountains.

G: How do you know that mountains cannot be moved? Have you ever tried?

L: Well, no.

G: Then take my word for it. Mountains can be moved, just as dust can be formed to create a new mountain. It's all just energy moved by thought.

L: Why does my inner voice sound like me and not someone else?

G: Because who is better to teach you than your own soul, who you have been since the beginning of time, as you created time.

L: When will I know it's not my inner voice but rather my ego?

G: When it does not come from love, it is not my words or actions.

L: You mentioned the Bible is not the whole truth. What about the Ten Commandments? Are they the whole truth?

G: Moses went up on the mountain by himself, but he also had lived in a body so his interpretation is accurate, but just as my words are not completely perfect here, they are not perfect there either.

L: So you are saying that what I am writing will not be perfect, yet when I asked you earlier, you said we could not write anything that was not meant to be written. So I am confused. How can this material help people if it's not 100 percent accurate?

G: Because it is how you interpret the information that matters most. This is why we say you must turn inward for the answers, as your soul will know the truth. Let us take the example of thou shall not kill from your Ten Commandments. This can be interpreted two ways: you may not murder or maim another being *or* you may not, under any circumstance, harm your own psyche and diffuse the senses so much that it would lead to a "death" of one's own body. Words are read, but words may not always be taken literally.

L: But what about the concepts?

G: The concepts come from love but also from what Moses expected would happen in his life as freer of the slaves. His actions were determined by the atrocities at hand, which he desperately wished to transform for himself and others. In his desperation, did he interpret our conversation. Can you see, then, why the concepts are not wholly perfect? It is not necessary to keep a holy day, for every day is holy. I do not require you to not take my name in vain. I do not ask you to be anything other than who you are, which is perfect and whole. The Ten Commandments can be interpreted as a road map to a life filled with gratitude.

L: OK, I think I understand. Can you give me another example?

G: Let's take thou shall not covet thy neighbor's wife.

L: I don't think it was written like that initially?

G: Aha, but was it not later interpreted that way?

L: I think so, yes.

G: In definition, the word covet would have meant "to desire earnestly," which we have just sent you to look up. And what happens when you desire something in earnest, as in "wanting it *real* bad"?

L: OK, that's funny how I heard you say in slang, "*real* bad."

G: We are funny.

L: Well, I have read in other spiritual books that the wanting of something only keeps it away because in our wanting are we telling the Universe to give us more "wanting" rather than give us what we . . .

G: Covet.

L: So the wording was correct; our interpretation was wrong?

G: Not wrong, misinformed.

L: OK, let's take one more just to really hammer this point home.

G: Thou shall not bear false witness.

L: What does that mean?

G: You tell me first your interpretation.

L: Don't tattle tale on your friends or neighbors or family members?

G: And why would you not do that?

L: Because seeing is not always believing? Oh, wait a minute. Don't believe everything you see! Is that the correct interpretation?

G: What you believe is what you will see. Bearing false witness creates more of the same. Don't believe everything you see is much more an accurate interpretation than your current theology suggests. Belief is the most powerful potion of the universe. Believe what you see, and you will see that which is true but that which is also untrue. Therefore, to not bear false witness allows for seeing more of the universal truths—that we are all one and the same and not separate and apart from God.

L: I get it, and I get now why you mean this message may not be perfect. It's not because what you are saying may not be true, but we should all be careful not to misinterpret the message.

G: Misinterpretation is a plague of many, many centuries and many, many, many men.

L: So we are busting down some massive religious doctrines here. What do I say when people tell me I am crazy?

G: You tell them you are.

L: Why?

G: Because no matter what you say, they will not hear you, for they will not be ready for the truth. Very few are ready for the truth, and that is why I must teach you and not others.

L: Is this because I am an old soul?

G: Partially, yes, but partially because you have evolved further than other spirits. If "old soul" will explain it to you, then that is OK with me. We will explain this further later on.

L: Are you male or female?

G: No.

L: Are you male and female?

G: I am both everything and nothing at all.

L: What does that mean?

G: It means I'm both here and not here.

L: Yeah. I'm still not understanding.

G: And you cannot, for it is a concept far beyond what the human mind can unravel save for someone as evolved as Albert Einstein. Later on, we shall attempt to explain in a manner for which you may understand. For now, we will continue with more simple questions.

L: OK. What do I need to do to become more godlike?

G: You need do nothing. You need only be.

L: Be what?

G: That which you say you want to be. We will explain this further in much detail later on in this material.

L: What happens when we die?

G: We go back to being who we really are.

L: Why can we not see those who have died?

G: The laws of the universe do not allow it.

L: What about people who see spirits?

G: Belief is of the mind, and therefore, what it sees with its own eyes cannot be questioned. However, this is not how we as cocreators have designed this system.

L: So there are no such things as ghosts?

G: No. Only stuck energy.

L: Can souls get stuck here?

G: Yes. Absolutely.

L: How can they get unstuck?

G: By recognizing who they are and why they came here just as you are here to remember.

L: Why do some people on earth learn this and others don't?

G: You cannot understand the scope of your magnificence and, therefore, cannot understand all the thoughts and beliefs others are thinking. I can assure you that anyone who thinks with the highest good thought is capable of blessing others with this same knowledge, which they already have. But does the system not work well the way we have designed it with some souls awake and some still asleep? This does not mean that everyone cannot wake up all at one time. Of course they can, but if they did, our magnificence would be revealed and forever would cease to exist on your planet. So it is not the way of the world for everyone to know everything, but they can if they want too.

L: Is Abraham in the *Law of Attraction* God? Is Esther channeling God?

G: She is channeling herself because she already knows the answers herself, just as you do. You all know the answers within.

All minds are connected and so you are all channels, in a sense. Some are just better at it than others, as you are, as she is.

L: Am I a messenger of God?

G: Do you think you are a messenger of God?

L: Yes and no.

G: Yes, why?

L: Because I have always felt different from other people.

G: And no, why?

L: Because all of this seems rather crazy and irrational and stupid that it's so incredibly easy.

G: It is easy for you. It is not easy for most people.

L: Why is it easier for me?

G: It is easier because you have been inspired by God, by Spirit, by the angels. You have lived many, many lifetimes always as a good person always wanting to know more. Why? Why? Why? Why? You have asked me so many times. Why do we hate each other? Why do we destroy each other? Why does the world have to be so corrupt and angry and terrible? Many times, you have died with these answers not being given, but now you have been here so many times in your existence that you cannot not know the truth, whereas others do not know or feel or comprehend what is the truth.

L: And what is the truth?

G: That you are a child of God. No more, no less than another human being on this planet or any other place in the universe (of which there are many). Humans are so funny in their beliefs of separation. They want to be the only thing out there, yet they are not. They are so pompous to believe there is nothing else or no one else in their existence. Yet I promise you there is.

L: Pompous does not seem like a word of God?

G: Laura is the one who places judgement upon the word. God seeks only to observe and report. For here you are asking me questions about the truth of the universe, and here we shall discuss and observe that which is happening all over your planet earth. Reserve judgement as you seek to inform your readers.

L: Will we find these other people?

G: Are they people? Yes, and yes, but not now, not for a really, really, really long time, but what does it matter? It's not as if you won't be there to see it! You will. Just not in the same body, for remember that time is eternal. You are eternal. All of us are eternal.

L: What should I do with this material?

G: Keep it for yourself until you are ready to share it.

L: With whom shall I share it?

G: The world, of course. But I will do that for you, this you must believe, but if you do not believe, then you will not share it.

L: I plan to share it.

G: And you will.

L: Am I a healer? I have been told this many times by mediums.

G: Yes.

L: Well, whom should I heal?

G: Anyone I send to you. I am already sending you souls, but you already know this, don't you?

L: I do. Yes. Whom have I healed?

G: No one and everyone, for we cannot know the effects of our healing unless we are able to see the results, but you know that the results are within their own minds.

L: How will I know if I have heard something wrong while I am listening to you?

G: Ask me.

L: Is anything wrong here?

G: Any and all words inscribed upon here by our healer (at the behest of God, spirit and angels) are accurate and true, at the time of the releasing of said material upon your planet earth.

L: What does inscribe mean in this context?

G: From our perspective, it means to write with God, spirit and the angels.

L: What can I do today to better understand all of this?

G: You need do nothing. I will take from you any thoughts as long as you will give them to me. Is there anything you wish to give to me now?

L: Oh my goodness, yes. I wish to give you my fear, doubt, worries, anger, resentment, frustration, fears about money, fears about love, fears about my age, fears about my children, fears about my parents . . . well, pretty much every thought that no longer serves me.

G: Are you done?

L: Yes.

G: Then it is done.

L: Is it that simple?

G: Simple practice. For each time, you activate your unlearning and unknowing of everything you think you have become; then too may you activate your remembering muscle of who you really are, which allows you to cocreate with God. This is what we would term prayer or intention. An undertaking of this simple practice is all one needs to begin a new course, sail a new boat, swim a new channel, or run a new marathon.

L: What am I meant to do with my life?

G: Do nothing. I will do it for you.

L: Well, how can we do nothing? Don't we have to take some action toward our prayers or intentions?

G: One need only understand one's relativity to the universe, i.e. one's relationship to the All That Is. If you are part (and apart) a portion of the All That Is, does it not make sense that when I say, "I will do it for you," that we are working toward your intentions together? So when I say, "Do nothing. I will do it for you," I simply need to say nothing means being. Be what it is you say you want to be. Be it. Live it. This is the nothing, "no thing," that will bring you what it is you are thinking that obtaining will fulfill your wanting, needing, or desiring.

L: But will it fulfill us? Doesn't happiness come from within? Aren't we supposed to desire nothing and just be happy?

G: And what would you do all day? Isn't life, physical life, for living out loud?

L: I guess so.

G: No. You know so.

L: Why are so many of us overweight? Why do we have terrible body images of ourselves?

G: Because you do not see the beauty that I see. You only see the body. If you saw through the body, into the soul, you would only see the magnificent being that you are.

L: Easier said than done. I really have a hard time with this, especially as I get older. My body is just not the same, and even though I don't eat poorly at all and go to the gym, I feel as if I am stuck in a cycle of—

G: Abuse. You are stuck in a cycle of abuse and self-denial and abject relativity to what the bodies function actually is for.

L: And what is the body for?

G: To grow and evolve one's soul. This is why the body changes form and shape and "ages." It is a necessary process of life. Though as humans you have made this process much quicker than it actually need be through the use of hormones and antibiotics in your food, consumerism, corporate brainwashing by scientific "facts." In other worlds, other realms, higher evolved souls use bodies much differently and therefore can extend their stay on that plane much longer. You humans have not evolved far at all. You are like little preschoolers running around the playground and bumping into each other. Some of you get up and cry and wail; others get up and laugh at how fun it all is and run around again and again. You can imagine most of you are crying babies on your planet, upset at the unfairness of life. You are like this sometimes. You go back and forth, up and down, over and back. You haven't yet learned to focus one's intention is a most powerful too. Stand in front of the mirror—go do it now—and declare, "I am a child of God. I am wholly perfect and beautiful. I need do nothing but declare my intention to always be ageless and magnificent and genius. Amen."

L: But how can that be all it takes? It honestly can't be that easy.

G: It is that easy, but what it is not is instantaneous. You are nowhere near a master of your universe, your domain (i.e. your own body and mind), and so you get caught up, caught back up, in the daily machinations of your mind: ugly, fat, out of shape, old, tired, unworthy, ill, misfortunate. Each and every time you think a thought that underserves your true nature, you activate the switch that keeps those lights on. How do you turn that switch off? Cocreating, in any instant, a new thought about yourself, such as the prayer we undertook, "I am wholly perfect and beautiful," is all one needs to do in any instant of self-denial. Turn to your mirror, and say it now.

L: I say it, but I don't believe it. I don't see that person you speak of in myself.

G: You can and you will if you were to undertake daily practice, daily intention of this principle. "I am wholly perfect and beautiful." Make it your mantra—daily, hourly, minute by minute if you have too—until you start to believe it.

L: I still feel as if it's easier said than done.

G: See a new you. Speak a new you, and a new you will emerge.

L: I will try, I guess.

G: You cannot trade in a life of despair for a life of deep, passionate being using the phrase "I guess." "*I Can* and *I Will.*" These are phrases of declaration willing the Universe to show you what it is you want to see in yourself.

L: Fine. I can and I will change my perception of my outer appearance.

G: Then it can and will be done unto you. As cocreators of the universe, we will all conspire to make your will ours.

L: So we do have helpers down here?

G: How do you know it's not up here? Down is a relative term. We are everywhere.

L: So then tell me about angels.

G: What would you like to know?

L: Do they exist?

G: Oh, very much so.

L: But what are they?

G: They are angels.

L: But what do they do?

G: Angels are guides who have lived many, many lives. They are here to help you as I am here to help you, as Jesus, the Christ, is here to help you, as Buddha and Gandhi and, dare I say it, even Hitler are here to help you.

L: Hitler? Are you kidding me? I would be crucified for writing that.

G: You hesitated to write it, but then you went back and did it anyway. Why do you think that is?

L: Because I know it's the truth?

G: Yes, because your soul does know the truth.

L: So how in the world would Hitler be here to help us?

G: This will not be popular to hear, but Hitler had only lived a few lifetimes (incarnations) before he came to be the man he was in Germany. As such, he had not known any of the rules of the universe, really, when he came into power. Some people know a little; they know enough to have compassion, empathy or even make general niceties with someone, but Hitler knew nothing of that. He lacked the capacity for any such notices, but what he had was charisma, charm, and the capability of making people follow him, just as Moses did. Do you hear me here? Hitler led the sheep to their slaughter because he lacked any empathy whatsoever. Moses, on the other hand, had lifetimes of knowledge and patience and compassion. Many, many lifetimes in fact, and a circumstance that allowed him to be who he truly was, freer of the slaves, maker of the laws of God (as he saw fit to disseminate them to the masses). The followers followed Moses because of the magnitude of his being. The magnitude of the being of Hitler was the same (though with an absence of any light whatsoever in his mind) and bound to a rule of the universe stating that which is like unto itself is drawn, his followers believed his rhetoric and rigmarole. Hitler knew only darkness and madness and mayhem.

L: OK, but come on now. Six million people died here. This is madness.

G: Is it madness or is it truth? Madness is someone who cannot see that what they are doing is wrong. Does this not happen every day in your world? Is a man who murders a child not just as mad as a man who murders an entire army, an entire race, an entire civilization.

L: So then go back to the part about Hitler being an angel?

G: I did not say that. I said he was a teacher, like Buddha. Has he not taught the world about peace and about how to treat (or not treat) your fellow man based on what he did? His teachings of what not to be are powerful beyond measure. Where would the world be had such a man not destroyed an entire species of its own kind? But you and I both know he only destroyed their bodies and minds, not their souls.

L: Meaning that the ramifications of his evil doing effected not only those who died but everyone as a whole?

G: Yes. I know this will not be popular to hear, but the collective consciousness created the mess and the martyr, the zealot and the sycophant.

L: I don't even know what the word sycophant means. I had to go look it up.

G: And did it apply here?

L: Yes.

G: Your world works the way it does because mass consciousness right now knows no other way to behave. There has not been a powerful teacher on a level as dark and scary and shocking as Hitler—

L: Until now?

G: Until now.

L: Are you speaking of Trump?

G: I am speaking of Trump. Has he not shined a light on the darkness of your country more so than any other leader? Look how far you have come, yet not far at all really. Trump himself is a teacher, but he, of course, does not know this, for only God can know the reasons Trump was made in a likeness that (beyond all measure) is almost, but not really, as dark a man as Hitler.

L: So is Hitler still a teacher? Is he hovering over us as a spirit?

G: Goodness, no. He is in another dimension learning other lessons, but he was a teacher to you and continues to do so in every classroom that ever seeks to teach the lessons learned from the Holocaust. His survival, in teachings of modern history, is what keeps many stuck in patterns of abuse. You cannot look toward the past to create a new future.

L: But earlier you said that Hitler is here to help us, like Buddha, so I don't understand how that is, as he was such a horrible man.

G: Horrible, yes, in your imagination that you have created about the world you see. Remember only love is real, and therefore, the Holocaust is not real from a spiritual sense, only from the realm in which you all live where whatever is not love is fake, is false, and is a mockery of reality.

L: Why did you not just say it is an illusion?

G: Because I know that is a word you do not enjoy. Therefore, I will use words that have meaning to you and only you. With others, I may use different words, but it is all the same.

L: So he is still a teacher to us. Why?

G: An event of such a magnitude is a reminder to always be better than you all were before. Thus, is his madness forever a teacher, as you are made to learn about history in your current school systems.

L: And you feel this is bad to continue rehashing the past?

G: We would not say bad, for this is a judgmental word and not one of true observation. We would merely say it might better serve you all to be taught differently rather than cohesively.

L: And what does that mean?

G: Don't let the sins of the past remind you of the future you have yet to create.

L: I still don't understand.

G: Probable cause.

L: Meaning?

G: Your future shall not be determined by past misgivings. Let bygones be bygones.

L: So forgive a man who murdered six million people? Uh, yeah. I don't think so.

G: This is why your world works the way it does, because so many believe in the false witness and illusion of mass murder and mayhem. One need only remember this falseness to remind oneself of their true nature, which is love, pure love.

L: There is no way our society can ever forgive a man who murdered six million humans. Nor can we forgive all those who turned a blind eye to it all.

G: But you can, and you must. A true spiritual being knows that which is true and that which is untrue. Look upon the untrue and declare it as such. Only then may you understand forgiveness is just.

I took a break from writing because this last exchange really threw me for a loop. I pondered if I should remove it, but when I listened to Conversations with God[8], *it too talked about Hitler, and I felt more at ease about leaving it in here. I resumed my questions a few days later.*

L: What is aging?

G: The body moving on. For what the body sees is that it cannot live forever, and it is, therefore, programmed to die off, eventually. How you take care of that body is entirely up to you, but at some point, your soul will leave that particular body and eventually, if you choose, come back into another one. This is what you all call "reincarnation."

L: Should we not call it that?

G: You may call it whatever you want. The word does not matter. The meaning is the same. To be born again, to learn again.

L: I thought we were here to remember and not learn though?

G: To re-mind oneself of that which one already knows. Could this not be called learning?

L: I guess so. Is it God I am talking to here or Spirit or something else?

G: It is all of us and none of us.

L: I don't get what you mean by none of us?

G: It is not you. It is not me. It is not any of us as separate entities. We all are of the same mind. Does that now make sense to you?

L: We think with the same mind. Therefore, I know everything you know, right? So what does it matter who is doing the talking?

G: Yes. Yes. Yes. You do it get it. I knew I picked a wise one.

L: Is this why I have felt different my whole life?

G: Explain different?

L: Smarter? More aware? I guess I would say more awake by having more common sense than most others, perhaps.

G: When you say it that way, you say it in a way that makes you separate. It is OK to say whatever you want, but different or special or unique or any other word that separates you from the masses is not correct. Jesus, the Dalai Lama, and Oprah Winfrey (to give you a modern-day reference) are no more useful or useless than you; what they have and what you have are minds that think like me.

L: Me being God?

G: Yes.

L: But you just said that we all think with the same mind?

G: We do, but that does not mean that everyone is thinking with right thinking when they come into body form. Right thinking is compassion, honor, commitment to goodness, and anything that inspires love. Those who think with love are never separated from the All of Everything. While you have not been perfect, you have since the dawn of time and even before that (since there is really no time at all) been one who sees our connection and honors civility and decency and common goodness. That means your mind is closer to mine. That is your specialness, as you called it, but it is not special at all, merely closer.

L: And what happens to those who choose to think mostly through fear?

G: Then it will feel as if they are separated from the whole, though they never truly are. This is the "illusion" of which we speak.

L: How can I help other people "wake up" and understand this?

G: Be my messenger. That is all you need do.

L: Can anyone talk to God in this way?

G: Those who are closer to my mind can and do all the time, but not everyone has evolved to a place of understanding that you and many others have.

L: Does Oprah talk to God?

G: Of course. All the time, but this you already know.

L: What makes someone famous? Are they chosen? Like J-Lo, was she chosen to be famous?

G: Not at all.

L: Was it not her destiny?

G: Fame is a human term to make special those who have aligned their thoughts with the magic that creates worlds.

L: I don't get it.

G: What is the magic that creates worlds?

L: Belief?

G: Yes. Belief. Belief in one's self is like dynamite on a stick. Once you harness the power of belief, you can create anything.

L: So J-Lo believes in herself so much that she created the life she has?

G: Yes, and in a God she believes so much in as well. She has not been perfect in this either. She has stumbled often, but she has also triumphed, and now she gets it right more often than not.

L: Can anyone be famous?

G: You already all are. To me.

L: Will I be famous?

G: Not at all. Do you want to be famous?

L: Not really. Not in the Hollywood sense.

G: And that is why you will not. Your soul knows your path, and it will give you exactly what you want.

L: I have no desire to be famous because I see what it does to people.

G: Which is why you will not be. You have willed yourself not to be.

L: I do wish to help others, though, but from a place of respect. I like the idea of being in front of an audience or a camera but only in a way that serves the highest good for all. I no longer wish to share stories that disempower. Can I inspire people with my words, these words?

G: That is up to you again, my dear. You can spend three, five, ten years asking me questions, but if this stays only with you, then no, you will not inspire with it. You know you are a good writer, but you know you cannot write like this. Only *you* and *I* and *we* can and that is why you must share it.

L: Why have I had so much insomnia lately?

G: You go to bed too late.

L: Is that a joke?

G: Yes. We do have a sense of humor, you know. The answer is that your soul is like the main act of a circus, waiting patiently from the sidelines to go on stage, and now that you are so near to the main entrance, your soul cannot contain itself.

L: I do believe in the concept of the mind-body connection and the mind creating all illnesses. So why can't I heal my skin?

G: You have asked this before in a different way. Your skin is a direct reflection of your innermost feelings and desires about yourself. Your desire is to be young, to be pretty, and to be ageless (as you keep praying about), but be honest. As you look upon yourself, you are not happy with the image that looks back in the mirror all the time. You do not like the flab, the sag, the wrinkles. You have yet to learn that the body image you reflect in the mirror has nothing to do with the body at all but with the mind.

L: Well, you just answered with the same answer told a different way.

G: Yes. Mind-body-soul are all connected. Look upon yourself in the mirror, and ask for a different result. Only then will you see your true beauty.

L: So give it to God to look upon?

G: Exactly.

L: Well, what would I say? My skin remains my biggest issue.

G: "Dear God in heaven, when I look upon myself, I see

imperfection. From now on, I allow and accept that which is perfect about me to shine through for all to see. Amen."

L: Tell me about *A Course in Miracles*[9].

G: It is a great book. I wrote it.

L: I thought Jesus or the Holy Spirit wrote it.

G: Yes.

L: So which of it is it?

G: It is all of us together. You, me, and everything in between. That is to say everyone. We all wrote it together because it is the truth. The truth is so easy to write, isn't it?

L: That's true because I have thought—

G: We know—

L: Many times of writing a book since my dad and brother died, a screenplay or a book about my life. But the thought of it is daunting, and so, therefore, I never do.

G: You should.

L: But I don't want to.

G: We know.

L: What do I want?

G: You want what you have always wanted: love, peace, harmony, and for people to be kind to one another, to share their souls.

L: I mean what do I want for my life?

G: Only you can answer that. I can only speak to what you want for your soul. Your life here on earth is what you make of it.

L: But how can I make my life better?

G: Get your thoughts about it in order.

L: How do I do that?

G: By thinking how I think. Is it not so simple? Yet you dummies on earth cannot get it together.

L: I don't think God would use a world like dummies.

G: But I just did. Didn't I? It is only a word. You are the ones who assign it meaning and judgement. It's funny. I do have a sense of humor, as I said earlier.

L: OK, well, then how can we stop being dummies?

G: Pay attention. Listen to my words. Use them. Don't abuse them by shoving them in a drawer somewhere or turning off the recording and going back to your regular, ho hum, mundane, everyday existence. There is a wealth of information for you; use it.

L: What is gut instinct?

G: Your most prized possession. The place of all knowing.

L: Is it always reliable?

G: Yes and no.

L: How do you mean yes and no?

G: No, it can't be trusted if your ego is doing the talking and listening. Yes, if it springs from a place of first knowing.

L: First knowing?

G: The first reaction you have to something is always the right reaction. The minute the ego gets involved, you are done for.

L: So we should go with our gut reaction?

G: Yes, as all thought stems from first thought.

L: What is first thought?

G: The reactionary pattern of all thought, where it all begins.

L: Can you elaborate?

G: First thought is the stem cells of the mind. It's where creation manifests everything.

L: Is the first thought always the right thought?

G: Yes, and yes! First thought is your inner most knowing about any subject at all that comes up.

L: So when we over analyze is when we start to fail?

G: Yes. The human mind cannot, will not, and should not overthink. The rational mind is the part of you whereby all good thought about a subject arises. The irrational mind, however, (or as you call it, the ego) is the place where dreams and illusions about the self come into being.

L: You mean the self that is the body?

G: Exactly. Precisely, my dear Watson!

L: I am kind of jumping all over the place; is that OK?

G: Of course.

L: How can I be a better parent to my son?

G: You ask this because you want the answer for all, not just yourself.

L: Yes.

G: Mindfulness. Being mindful of their wants, needs, desires, fears, doubts, and worries and knowing when to help. As parents, we help too much, but does this concept of mind-body-soul not apply to children as well? Do you not know they are here to remember who and what they are as well?

L: And how can we help them to do this if you say we help too much?

G: Sit back and observe. Be an observer of their experience. If they are shy, let them be shy. If they are loud and proud and crazy exuberant, let them be that too. We will return to this subject later in more detail and in other books and materials.

L: Is there such a thing as soul mates?

G: Yes, we are all soul mates.

L: But I mean in terms of love?

G: Same answer.

L: OK. Well, let me ask it this way. There have been a hundred thousand books, songs, TV shows, articles, and movies written about love in terms of a life partner or soul mate. So is there such a thing as the perfect person out there for each of us?

G: This answer will burst the bubble of so many, but the real answer is that no there is not a "perfect person," as you say. We are all soul mates. So, in a sense, we are all perfect partners to each other, but to answer your question in human terms, no. There are a million perfect people out there for you.

L: So why do we want a soul mate so badly?

G: Because love is the most powerful feeling in the world, and if your soul knows this, then it makes sense to be wanting a partner of love and romance. Isn't romance grand? I invented it.

L: I don't remember anymore.

G: You will.

L: Well if we have a million perfect partners, then why is it so hard to find just one, and why is it even more difficult to keep one?

G: It is for you. It might not be for some. It all depends on the personality or, again, the ego.

L: Well, clearly my ego is a problem for me when it comes to love. I suck at it.

G: You do not. You are perfectly capable of having a loving relationship.

L: So what is stopping me?

G: You are stopping you.

L: Why?

G: You are a wanderer and always have been. In 772 lifetimes, you have not yet learned what you need to learn about love.

L: And what is that?

G: That it can be forever. That it can be eternal, because it is. The ego part of you is so overcome with wanting something else better.

L: I'm listening. Go on.

G: Are you sure you are ready?

L: Yes.

G: Your ego wants what it cannot have.

L: And what is that?

G: Eternal love from a partner who wants to be with you forever. In every lifetime, you have been hurt and discarded by someone close to you. Rather than being hurt again, you discard them first, like a cheap pair of shoes that have worn out at the toes.

L: But why can't I learn the lesson?

G: Because you have not asked me to help you, ever. Until now. Are you wanting my help here with this? I feel your fear right now in your stomach.

L: Yep.

G: That is OK. That is why I am here; that is why I am always here in every instant you need me.

L: So what do I say or do to transform what clearly is a lifetime's worth of pain?

G: Give it to God or the Universe or whatever word works for you. Say "Dear God, Universe, all-powerful, all-knowing being of light. I cannot seem to know what it is to be a loving partner to another being of light. Take from me the sorry and sorrow I carried with me throughout lifetime after lifetime so that I may be free of the burden of not knowing how to love a man or a woman as a man or a woman. Amen."

L: Is it odd that right after we wrote that, fireworks literally went off outside my bedroom window? *(It is the day before the Fourth of July.)*

G: It is not odd at all. There is no coincidence my dear. 772 lifetimes is a long time to wait for salvation.

L: So now what? Do I just wait for Mr. Right to waltz through my door? Is it that easy?

G: There is no Mr. Right or Mr. Wrong. There are only the people you draw into your experience based on your thoughts, words, and action.

L: So is this why I got divorced?

G: Yes. Many of your relationships have come to an end over this issue. You have also strayed in relationships that no longer served your ego in times when divorce would have resulted in being shunned or worse.

L: You mean in other lifetimes? Is this why I have been a single mother?

G: Yes. Twelve times you have had to navigate the world of children by yourself.

L: Back-to-back?

G: Not back-to-back, but some more recent than others.

L: Have I been someone in my lineage before on earth?

G: Yes.

L: Can you say who?

G: Yes.

L: So who have I been?

G: Someone who is sitting next to you right now. Do you know her name?

L: No. Do you? Wait, Evelyn?

G: And who is Evelyn?

L: I have no idea.

G: Come on. Give it a think. Picture her. In your mind, you will see her.

I closed my eyes and saw an image of a woman sitting in a chair looking out the bay window of a brownstone.

L: She was a caretaker, a lover of children. Her life was cut short because she fell gravely ill. The depths of her sorrow were too much. She had been left behind by a man. He was cruel to her and unkind. He too did not know how to love eternally. She sat at the window of her house every day willing that he would come back to her, but he never did.

G: Did they have children?

I closed my eyes again.

L: I don't think I can get it.

G: You can, and you will. We all have the ability to see into the past, present, and yes, even future. Some of us are just better at it than others. Go on. Try again.

L: Jerry and Evelyn were married in 1927 and had no children. They met at a high school dance. He walked her to school every day. He became an architect, and she was a teacher. Her longing for children is what kept her from ever having them. Her longing for children is what kept her from experiencing everlasting love. Her deep sorrow is what pushed Jerry away.

G: Does this sound familiar?

L: Very. So are we destined to repeat the same mistakes over again?

G: There are no mistakes, as you say, but yes, you will continue to have the exact same experiences repeatedly as you navigate through each lifetime.

L: So what is my issue with children?

G: A deep sense of longing carried over between two lifetimes.

L: How can I get over this?

G: Get over what?

L: The longing for more children.

G: When you were Evelyn, you came to me and prayed over it many times.

L: I thought prayer was the medium of miracles? So why did she not have children?

G: The desire never went away. She could not manifest the having into being. The not having was so torturing her that she could not see my miracles.

L: Did you send her signs or messages?

G: Many, many times.

L: And what happened?

G: I told you she could not see nor hear them in her wanting-ness. Therefore, there was no having-ness.

L: Can you explain that further?

G: Wanting a thing only serves to keep it away from you, as you are alerting the Universe of the fact you want something, which is, in fact, a statement of lack. Quit wanting; begin accepting and behaving in a way that shows gratitude for that which you already are and have. Everything you ever want or need already exists as possibility. Therefore, there is never a need to ask for it as if you don't have it. Simply accept it fully as your truth and your having-ness begins to take shape.

L: I am not sure I quite grasp that concept yet.

G: You will. Your eternal nature requires it.

L: If we are eternal, then why do our bodies age?

G: We do not age. Only our bodies do so.

L: Can we stop this?

G: Yes. There is a way to stop this body process of aging and shedding our outer most being, but you humans are not capable of such an undertaking.

L: Why not?

G: Your thoughts are too deeply embedded right now on the process of living and dying. For you cannot understand how I created the body not to slough off and wither and die. You can only hear and see what medical science has shown to be the process of eliminating the body from the mind and soul.

L: Which is what?

G: The pain of dying need not happen the way it does. The function of the body is to live, not die or mutate diseases. I have told you diseases are of the mind not the body. Yet most do not believe it.

L: So we don't need to get wrinkles?

G: Are wrinkles a bad thing?

L: Well, yes.

G: And thus, the ego has reared its ugly head.

L: What's wrong with wanting to be beautiful?

G: You are beautiful. You are all beautiful creatures of God and the Universe. If you could just see yourself the way I see you, we would not be having this conversation about wrinkles or sags or any other nonsensical view of your perfection.

L: OK, I get it.

G: You do, but you still do not see yourself the way I see you, a most beautiful creation just like all of my other creations.

L: I liked the story about Evelyn. Can you tell me about any of my other past lives?

G: Can you?

L: Ugh. OK, I get it. I don't need you for that.

G: No. You do not. But I will indulge you for one more. Are you ready?

L: Yes.

G: You have been an Indian Princess, which I know you have been told on many prior occasions by other healers. You lived in a tribe of many, many other healers who took the sick and the dying and made them well. But one day, a plague came to your tribe that you could not contain. The women all died. The men all died. Only the healers lived.

L: Why did only the healers live?

G: They had only enough medicine.

L: I have been told that I took care of the children after the mothers died.

G: That is true.

L: Why did the children not die?

G: Some of them did. Your son was your son then too. He also has lived many, many lives with you.

L: How many children lived?

G: Fifteen.

L: Why is this hard to write?

G: Because of your soul, which knows this is the truth and wants to release it with you here now.

L: This is very painful. I feel this very deeply at my core.

G: You have carried this for far too long.

L: How long?

G: A millennium.

L: A thousand years?

G: Yes, give or take one hundred.

L: So what do I need to do to heal the pain?

G: You need do nothing at all. I will do it for you.

L: How?

G: If you are ready, I will tell you what to say.

L: I am ready.

G: "Dear Bringer of light and Keeper of peace, please take from me this overwhelming sadness that I have carried for nearly eleven hundred years. I cannot know the depths of despair that have followed me so intensely, but I know now that it was not my fault. This was a plague of the mind of mass consciousness of my tribe. Bringing man's tools into the land caused anger and resentment among the leaders. Their harsh bitter treatment led our hearts astray. It was not my intention to live while they died, but it was my soul's intention to be among the living, and so I did. Their children became my children, and for this I hold much guilt and grief. For I cannot stand to see a motherless child, now or ever. I know now that I cannot save nor fix everyone or everything, and so I ask, dear God, to be healed."

L: And that will work?

G: Do you not feel better?

L: A little, I guess.

G: It is a process, and you will feel as you move through other lifetimes that this heavy burden has been removed.

L: Why did I push you away for so long? What was my issue with God?

G: You had no issue with God, as a concept, merely an issue with organized religious institutions teaching ungodly things.

L: Like?

G: Vengeance and damnation and fear.

L: Yeah that seems about right. Where do I go from here?

G: Wherever you want. The world is your oyster as they say.

L: Even with talking to you and feeling confident this is the truth, some of this is still so hard to get and to believe. For instance, why am I still so hung up on money?

G: I sent you a song today. Did you not get it?

L: "Have a Little Faith in Me." I got it.

G: Did you believe it?

L: Very much so. I laughed, didn't I?

G: That you did.

L: Why is faith so hard for me? For all of us?

G: Because you are trusting in yourself.

L: Isn't that who I am supposed to trust?

G: No silly. What have you been doing for the last two years?

L: Waking up?

G: And what have you been learning and unlearning?

L: To trust in a power greater than just me?

G: To trust in a power greater than you, greater than all of you. It is the sum of all parts. It is God. It is Universal Presence. There is no thing to trust in other than *You* and *Me. We.* Trust in *We.*

L: So don't just think, "Oh, God will bring it to me if I pray for it"?

G: Prayer only works when it comes coupled with belief. Let me say that again because it is so important. *Prayer only works when it comes coupled with belief.* And do you believe that you can create the life you want?

L: Not really.

G: Then we have much more work to do here.

L: I will get there.

G: And you will. For you are now remembering. Little by little, step by step, you will indeed get there. We will go there together *You* and *Me* and *We.*

L: Is there something I could say to help?

G: I am.

L: That's it?

G: I am abundant. I am capable of creating wealth and abundance in all areas of my life. The power of "I am" cannot be overstated. I am. I am. I am. I am.

L: Can you say I am not?

G: Miscreation.

L: Message received.

G: I am knowing. I am creation. I am love. I am happiness. I am joy. I am so full of wonder and excitement about the future that I cannot wait until tomorrow.

Since I began having this conversation with God, I had been staying up very late, and so sometimes I would just take my computer and write, but on this particular night the computer turned on but would not open the document. I tried again, and something else went wrong. My thought was that it was not a good time to write right then. I tried to quiet my mind, but nothing happened. I felt as if it was not the time for asking but rather for listening.

G: You are correct.

L: So you are there?

G: Of course. I am always here.

L: I think I get my problem here. Fear is holding me back. Fear of retribution. Fear of failure. Damn fear. It sneaks up on you in unexpected ways. I know that I have to write the beginning of this book, and I fear that now too.

G: And we can help you with that.

L: You are back. Where have you been?

G: Waiting for you to find what it is you needed to proceed. Do you wish to go to bed now?

L: Not yet.

G: Then let's proceed with your questions, and I will proceed with the answers. Do you have a question?

L: I'm having fear.

G: Fear of what?

L: Fear of going forward.

G: And of what are you afraid?

L: No one will believe me.

G: Let me take care of that.

L: No one will care.

G: Let me take care of that.

L: No one will understand.

G: I understand.

L: You do?

G: Yes.

L: Dear God, please take from me these fears of moving forward with this book so that I may share your truth, our truth.

G: Sound the trumpets. You are learning. Shall we go on?

L: Where am I not being loving and kind?

G: Well, first of all, to yourself. You are very hard on yourself.

L: I know.

G: Let's fix that.

L: How?

G: Let's begin with asking.

L: What would I say?

G: "Oh, Keeper of the universe, all that is divine, I know that I am divine too. I only ask that I am allowed to see my divine goodness in all its beautiful and perfect glory. Amen."

L: Why do we say amen?

G: I don't know. You all made it up, but I like it.

L: Then I guess we should keep it.

G: Indeed.

L: What about "and so it is"?

G: Also good. There are so many ways to wrap it up. I'd even take a wink.

L: A wink?

G: Sure, why not. A nod, a secret handshake, whatever works. You have more questions but you are getting tired.

L: It's hard to sleep.

G: Sleep is important, for when we rest we recalculate.

L: Why did I get pregnant with my son? I was thirty-eight years old, and doctors told me I had a 5 percent chance of getting pregnant after thirty-five. Why did it end up being with someone who decided not to be a part of his life?

G: Let's take the first question. Your will to get pregnant was stronger than your will not to get pregnant.

L: Yes. But you have said that wanting something too much keeps the things you want away.

G: Did I say you wanted it?

L: No.

G: I said you willed it to happen. Your will is stronger than your wanting because wanting is the deepest darkest parts of your personality (or ego) that you (as the you who you presently are) mostly keep hidden, even from yourself.

L: I don't follow.

G: What you wanted was a baby. What you willed was a soul, the soul who is most close to you in this universe, your son. Your connection with him is strong.

L: I think I am still lost.

G: Well, think of it like this. To you he felt like a wanting, a longing for a child, a family. To your soul he is and was your equal. You have been together so many times that it feels as if no time has passed between lifetimes. Yet as a body, it has. Your soul had been searching for a while to have him return you to the feeling of being together. At the place where you had been, it was not possible for you, the body, and you, the soul, to come to an agreement.

L: On what?

G: On what you wanted. You, the body, wanted a child and husband and family. You, the soul, had reason to believe that your child's soul had not chosen this circumstance from which to grow and evolve. Meaning his soul wanted an incarnation, unlike any other, which allowed for him to not have this particular father figure permanently. Therefore, it made the decision to advance your soul by bringing to you a child that had no father, not unlike other lifetimes before this one.

L: Was there any way to stop that from happening?

G: Your free will.

L: But I did not use that.

G: No. You did not.

L: Will my son and his biological dad reunite ever?

G: That is the plan, should free will not get in their way. Each has a choice to make either from the soul or the ego. But again, you have a knowing that answers already for you.

L: Yes. I do.

G: Do you not want that?

L: I want what is best for my son.

G: As does he. Are you understanding yet?

L: Sort of.

G: Your will to live is stronger than your will to die because dying is not really possible. Therefore, the will that is love is always creating.

L: I get it now.

G: We knew you would.

L: My soul's will for us to be back together came from love. My wanting of a child came from fear. Fear of being alone?

G: Tremendous.

L: Do I want more children?

G: Only you can answer that.

L: Sometimes I feel as if I do, but other times, I am scared of starting over.

G: Because of your age?

L: Yes.

G: Fear. Your physical capabilities?

L: Yes.

G: Fear. Your ironclad agreement stating you are going to be alone forever.

L: Perhaps.

G: Fear. And what is your will?

L: To connect.

G: Connect with?

L: Connect with the part of me that feels missing.

G: And from where does that come?

L: The soul.

G: Aha.

L: Aha. So does that mean there are other souls?

G: Many. Some closer than others. The parent-child relationship is by far the strongest. And what may I ask holds you from being with these other souls?

L: Nothing.

G: Nothing but fear. False Evidence Appearing Real. I will put some love into your mind. Close your eyes, and tell me what you see.

L: Me in a hospital bed holding a baby.

G: And does your rational mind know this is possible.

L: Not at all. Too old. Too scared. Too lonely.

G: And from where do all of those thoughts stem?

L: Fear.

G: Shall we pray on it?

L: Yes.

G: "Oh, how I pray, dear Father, that the false evidence of my infertile body be shown to you so that any and all notions that are not for my highest good be removed. Amen."

L: I think part of our infertility crisis stems from how we are treating our environment right now. What are we doing to our planet right now?

G: You are destroying it, piece by piece, little by little.

L: And how can we fix that?

G: By being more godlike. Seeing the planet the way I see it, as the beautiful, wondrous creation that I have created with you. You thought I was going to say for you, didn't you?

L: I did.

G: What is wondrous to me is how you can consume animals and know nothing of how that affects not only the body but also the planet as a whole. Do you think I put animals here for consumption, or do you think that perhaps they came here as you came here, for atonement?

L: Do animals have souls?

G: Of course they do.

L: Other animals eat other animals though.

G: Yes, and that is by design.

L: Why?

G: To sustain life.

L: But if humans can survive without eating meat, why can't some of the animals who eat other animals?

G: There is no good answer on this other than to tell you that we each have a role to play in the universe. Animals are no less important to the evolutionary function of our planet.

L: Why not our universe?

G: Animals do not live on every planet.

L: Are they only on Earth?

G: Not necessarily.

L: What about plants? Should we be eating those?

G: All the time. Only plants are capable of giving you the nourishment the bodies, which I have created with you, are needing.

L: Do plants have souls?

G: Not in the way that you do, but yes, on the evolutionary scale they do.

L: What of all the hormones and pesticides and drugs we put into our food. Everything gives you cancer now?

G: And whose fault is that?

L: All of ours.

G: Exactly. Do you think that I would want that for you all?

L: No.

G: Do you feel that this is God's way of punishing?

L: I don't.

G: Yet many do.

L: True.

G: Do you see my point?

L: That the mass consciousness is why we are all so sick?

G: Yes.

L: Let me ask the question many have been asking for centuries. What is the meaning of life?

G: To love and be loved.

L: But you have told me we are here to evolve.

G: Is being evolved not love?

L: What do I say when some scholars, scientists, and theologians dismiss all of this as having been written by someone with "an active imagination"? Because you know they will.

G: Yes, this is possible. Say nothing. Do nothing. For all who come to read and relate to this material are understanding of your intentions to enlighten and heal, not to alarm and misinform.

L: OK, well, I listened today to *Conversations with God, Book Two*[10] and nearly fell on the floor when we started talking about Hitler. Why did I just write "we"!?

G: Because you can't not know the truth. We are we. And basically, you heard a similar truth told in words that had meaning to you.

L: Yes.

G: Do you see how this works? You ask. I answer every time.

L: I think I was so shocked because it is as if I am not writing the words. They come into my head, and I am baffled by how that is happening. The name of Hitler being juxtaposed with Gandhi or Buddha seems so crazy, but when I go back to read what we wrote, it makes sense. It is surreal.

G: Yet does is not make sense, all of it? Are you not a divine being, a creature who has communed with us for all of eternity?

L: There is still fear.

G: We know.

L: Why?

G: Because all of this makes for a world that will now be hard for you to live in. You are now ready for resurrection.

L: Meaning?

G: That life as you know it has changed from thinking about your next dollar, your everyday, mundane, ho hum existence, and has morphed into the whole divine nature of your being. You have the tools now.

L: The tools for what?

G: To be. To just be.

L: Be what?

G: To be all that you are and all that you have ever been.

L: So many questions.

G: So many answers.

L: Do we really live simultaneous lives? Are there parallel universes?

G: There is no thing that you cannot do, be, or have, so why do you get so hung up on time and space?

L: Because it is all we know.

G: Is it? I have sent you many, many messengers of science to disprove all of this.

L: So where do we go? Are you saying there are other mes at all times?

G: Well, yes and no.

L: Oh, Lord.

G: You do make me laugh. Do you want an answer? All roads lead to one place, right back here to me, to God, but we all have many, many, many routes and destinations along the way. You have I-95. You have the turnpike, the backcountry roads, the long way, and the short way, but are they not all leading to the same place? It's as if you are on a bus while another you is on a plane. Another yet still is riding a horse and buggy or walking to your destination. Are you not all racing to the same destination? Yet somehow you have no idea the other is just as determined to get there as well.

L: That is the yes part, but what is the no?

G: No is that you cannot yet know how it all ends. So each part of you plans how to survive from a standpoint of not knowing. Go with me here—

L: You mean the soul plans each path, yes?

G: There are yous in every part of the universe. Each has a job to do, which is to advance your soul.

L: Do we all look exactly the same?

G: Certainly not.

L: I am getting frustrated and lost.

G: Put your ego aside.

L: I'll try.

G: No one body is exactly the same, just as no one star or snowflake is the same. You are perhaps a different type of body on another plane. There are other worlds where bodies look very different from yours.

L: I have heard this.

G: And it is the truth.

L: It's hard to believe.

G: Am I not the creator of all life?

L: Yes.

G: Do you think I have only one pen with which to write, one stroke from which to swing?

L: I guess not.

G: I have created many types of worlds and yours is just one microcosm in a vast multiplex of unimaginable joy.

L: I'm still confused by the simultaneous lives. So every life is happening all at the same time?

G: Yes and no.

L: What is the yes?

G: All lives are happening at once.

L: And the no?

G: All lives may not be advancing as every part effects the whole, so all thoughts, words and actions are in direct correlation of thoughts, words and actions in others lifetime's circumstances and creations.

L: So everything in every lifetime effects the whole depending on what we are doing in that lifetime?

G: Yes.

L: What type of things would affect whether or not other lives advance?

G: Having a baby, having a cancer, having a problem which persists and remains unsolved. These are just the many ways in which all lifetimes are connected to one another.

L: I would imagine the problems we hold onto are also at issue here as well?

G: Yes. Absolutely. This is how it can be explained that whenever one who seeks to know God completely and fully has reached a state of awareness with the All That Is, that all lifetimes are effected. Waking up in your current lifetime reverberates through all the others, creating a ripple effect which causes a chain reaction making all lives easier and some unnecessary. For once you have completed your task of knowing, you are set free in another lifetime. Does this make sense to you?

L: I think so.

G: You will have a think on it and we shall return to this topic later.

7

God—The Interview, Part Two

"Dear God, I accept that although my mind has wandered off, I may return at any given moment to my source. I accept that as we write here together again, the words flow freely and effortlessly. Amen."

Laura: What does intention bring?

God: Intention brings all that you have desired to the forefront of your mind. Not unlike a goal, its sets the dialogue so that creation may begin to take hold.

L: Is it necessary?

G: It is a tool. Think of it like a Sharpie, a permanent marker indicating what you wish to create in a clear, defined, nonerasable way.

L: I am still shocked how easily words come out when I am writing.

G: You know the words as I do; that is why it is such an easy dialogue. We write together not separate. Separation is not possible remember. You have a fervor now for this material, no?

L: Absolutely. I don't want to stop or put the computer down! How should we spend each day?

G: Consistently being in the space of awareness.

L: Awareness of what?

G: Of all that you are and all that I am. Of how to keep peace and joy, as you all say you want.

L: And how is that?

G: Consistent awareness of Love's presence in your life as a body.

L: Why as a body?

G: The soul knows only joy and love. The body and mind separated have a harder time with this concept and, therefore, must be consistently taken out for a spin. If a car sits in a garage not used, its motor will not function properly. Maintenance is the key to anything. Whatever you ignore will then start to wither and eventually die off.

L: Wow. I start to write, and I have no idea where we are going with it, and then it takes off and makes complete sense.

G: It is so simple. Yet there are those who cannot, will not, let go of their theologies and traditions and nonsensicalness.

L: Why do we have so many different theologies?

G: There is no one right way to know God. Only you can decide which is right for you. The best option is the one that works within the context of who you are at the core, from the ego perspective, because who you truly are is Spirit.

L: But from what I have learned these last few years, the ego is not the truth, it sees only illusion.

G: Yes, but the ego does not know this, and therefore, while you are in the body form, you are learning from a place of body. Children do not yet have the capability to discern between mind, body, and spirit, and so it is from their ego where they decide all decisions about religion.

L: But what about adults?

G: Adults have been programmed from a young age as well to accept or believe what they have been told about God and the Universe. Although, most religions do not speak of the Universe; they speak only of the theology of God.

L: What about Muslims?

G: Same. Their theology is no less right or wrong than the rest of religion, be it Christianity, Catholicism, Buddhism, Judaism, Islam, Hinduism, and so on and so forth. It all comes from wrong-minded thinking.

L: But you just said that the theology is no less right or wrong.

G: Wrong-minded thinking and right and wrong are two separate ideas. In wrong-minded thinking, you are thinking from a place of ego or body or separation. To think with and from Love is the only right perception. Being right or wrong implies a judgement, and God does not judge. Therefore, each religion's theology is not wrong or right. I do not care which choice you decide upon when it comes to God, only that you decide for and with God.

L: But what of religions that teach the wrath of God or that God's vengeance will rain down upon you if you are a bad person?

G: Concepts like those come only from the mind of mankind. They are not of God. They never were or never will be. There is no vengeance for mistakes, because mistakes are simply the illusion of separation from God.

L: So what is real?

G: Only Love.

L: Why do I always capitalize the word Love. It's as if my hand refuses not too when I type.

G: Because it is the most powerful, most all-encompassing, most bombastic, most fantastic, most stupendous, most courageous thing to be, give, and have. Does it not deserve some adulation with capitalization?

L: Well, when you put it that way, then yes. Love deserves

L. Why is it so hard to grasp these concepts but not be fully living them right now?

G: All that you are is all that you will ever be, and therefore, our ego fights for survival. For it knows that once you let go of ego, there will be no use for it.

L: So what happens?

G: What happens is pain and sorrow will continue to come about until you have borrowed enough time, in time and space, to get to the other side of knowing and faith.

L: Borrowed time?

G: All humans are on borrowed time in your plane of existence—the time and space of earth, as there is no time and space in the kingdom of heaven.

L: Is there a heaven?

G: Indeed. You are living in it right now.

L: It doesn't seem like heaven.

G: Well, close your eyes, and let me show you.

I closed my eyes.

G: Now write down what I have shown and told you.

L: You said to me, "Do you not have a beautiful home? Do you not have your son, your mom still with you? Do you not have the trees, the mountains, the oceans, the air you breathe, the oxygen of life?" I can understand that, but it certainly does not feel like heaven here on earth most days. In fact, for many, if not most people, it can feel like hell.

G: And it will become your job to teach people that it is not the case. It only feels like hell because you are trapped within the confines of the ego mind, where no good thoughts live. If thoughts are what create the reality you see, does it not make sense that you see only hell right now? Trade the attack or hate thoughts of yourself, your people, your government, your money system, your corporate pharmaceutical system, your food system, your welfare and poverty system, and your jobs system, and all of the wrong-minded thinking confines in which your humans of Earth live, and you will begin to see that hell has come to your society only by means of the ego mind. The way back to heaven is to follow us through faith and transformation to only what is real, and that is what with a capital L?

L: Love.

G: Yes. Love will maintain a sense of well-being and commune with God and heaven, but your people are not ready for this. They have not been ready for millions of moments or thousands of what you call years.

L: And why is that?

G: We need more messengers. We need more soldiers in the fight for Love's survival. Soldiers whose only weapons are the peace and Love of God and who are willing to share each and every day a message that most human beings do not, cannot, and will not take in because fear is so pervasive on your planet.

L: Well, how can only a few save billions?

G: Because thoughts of God are shared from one to the other. For every godlike thought, a million more minds meet up with it. When you bless a stranger (an unknown ego mind) the thought then ricochets like a laser beam into the minds of other beings. A shared thought is like a shark who feeds off the tiny minnows. All those tiny fish get gobbled up in just one fell swoop.

L: I love your analogies and metaphors. Sometimes I start writing and have not a clue what any of it means until I finish.

G: We feel your fear as you write. You need to let go of that sense of things not making sense, for they always do.

L: Speaking of sharks. What do you think of the family the Kardashians?

G: I do not think of them any differently than I think of you all.

L: But they are so famous and such a huge part of our society right now.

G: And of what would you say they teach?

L: Nothing good.

G: Really?

L: They do nothing charitable that I know of and seem to think only of themselves. Yet the young generation wants to be just like them. Young people want the money, the fame, the cars, and all the materialism that comes with being famous.

G: Is that not a form of teaching though? This family cannot and will not stop the creation train they are on. In their giving back (and they do, trust me), they are bringing forth more and more for themselves. Just because they don't speak of charity does not mean they are not charitable. And as for the teaching part, their wealth and status do not come without the strings of humanity attached: judgment, condemnation, and harsh words spoken by strangers (and seekers of fame and the same things they have). There is a pervasive sense in your society that to be rich and famous is the be-all and end-all, but I can tell you it is not. Unless and until they change their minds about who and what they really are, there will come a time when future generations will look back and remember this family as great leaders who simply failed to remember that life is about giving not getting.

L: But you just said they do give.

G: Monetarily absolutely. Do they share love and kindness and grace and understanding, or do they share images of unattainable concepts and creations that for all intents and purposes harm our children's way of thinking?

L: Then what are they teaching?

G: To obtain is to remain in chains. To acquire is to perspire.

L: I still don't think I understand how they are teachers

because the truth is millions upon millions of people are obsessed with them and many other famous people.

G: What do all famous people have in common?

L: Lack of privacy?

G: Lack of *love.* Fame and adulation are not love. They are forms of deceit and denial of one's own power to create.

L: So we look to others who are rich and famous and then think we cannot have what they have? So, therefore, we are powerless?

G: Exactly. This is the lesson of all celebrity: to love thyself and know that no one is more special or unique than anyone else. Until this is learned, we will continue to send you false gods. Adulation is not of God. It is of ego.

L: Again, this whole thing had me frustrated, but now that we are finished, it makes perfect sense. Yet the word "teacher," which you have used many times for people I don't feel are teaching us, is bothersome to me. Shouldn't the word teacher be used to define someone who is helping and not hurting us?

G: A lesson learned is a lesson learned whether it comes from a space of love or fear. To teach is to remind people of that which they already know (or don't believe they know, even though in actuality they know more than they can comprehend in their current lifetimes). A teacher of truth seeks to inform. A teacher of wisdom seeks to enlighten. A teacher of force seeks to punish. A teacher of pain seeks to harm. A teacher of principles teaches true knowledge. Do you see how teacher can mean both things?

L: Teachers are not always people who are showing us great things but also those who may be teaching us harmful things?

G: Also, who unknowingly or subconsciously are shining a light on atrocities and attrition.

L: You say you will use words that I know, yet there have been many words I don't recognize when we are writing.

G: For this is by design so you may know and recognize that which is truth and that which is of ego and remove it accordingly. Reading and writing exactly as you are capable of doing, as the current inscriber, is not an indication of who is dictating said material. Words may be difficult, and for this we are sorry, but here we are trying to show you we are cocreating not simply as you but as the Oneness. *You* and *Me* equals *We,* as we have said before.

At this point in our dialogue, it is starting to feel as if I am talking to an old friend. I tried to keep my own personal issues out of the topics, but one question had been weighing heavily on my mind. I prayed about it before I went to bed.

L: I have been thinking about adoption again. Well, at least I was last week.

G: And now?

L: Now I am maybe back to putting it on hold.

G: We prayed on it, did we not?

L: Yes.

G: Thus, why you have placed it on back burner.

L: So is that what I need to be doing?

G: Let's pray on it now, shall we?

L: OK.

G: "Dearest Father in heaven and Keeper of all children, please allow me to know what is truly in my heart and soul when it comes to bringing my eternal life partners into this plane of existence. For my ego cannot, and does not, know the right path for my soul. Only you know, and therefore, we must decide together if they are to be with me or not. Amen."

L: And now what?

G: We will stop here.

I went to bed and thought about it the next day.

L: I took some time and thought about it and realized that again fear is my stopping point. All the fears we spoke of before. Age. Money.

G: Did we talk about money fears in relativity to more children?

L: I think so.

G: We did not.

I went back through the material to see if this was true.

L: You are correct. I went back to look, and I did not bring up money.

G: Of course I am correct. I am God.

L: So yes, money is a huge, major stumbling block for me when it comes to adoption or any other means of having more children.

G: And why do you feel this is so?

L: Because I don't have the financial means to just waste my money should an adoption fail again, nor do I really have the money for it. Nor do I have the money to have the help it would take to raise a baby on my own again.

G: Wow. That is a fair amount of stumbling blocks for you.

L: It is. I know.

G: What is fear?

L: False evidence appearing real.

G: Do you not know that all financial means and a path will be paved with and for you by God and Spirit?

L: I still lack faith.

G: Yes.

L: I still have fear and lack of trust in God to deliver me out of my own human mind.

G: Yes.

L: And how may I fix this?

G: Give it to God. It is the only way out of the mental patterns keeping you in the cyclical nature of your own life.

L: It does feel like a cycle.

G: Shall we pray?

L: Yes.

G: "Oh, Father, I cannot know what is best for me. My own pervasive thoughts have gotten me to where I am now and where I have always been, stuck in a cycle of self-abuse and condemnation. Please release me from these patterns of denial of my own power within and the power of God within. Amen."

L: That's it?

G: That's it.

L: It's that simple?

G: Yes. It is. Consistency, though, is paramount in all thoughts that meet up with God's. Therefore, the only way to know the truth is to live it moment after moment after moment after moment, as we have said before.

L: Easier said than done. Is it possible to ask God's opinion on something?

G: No, for that is not how the communication link works. We are not your gossipy girlfriend sitting down for a spot of tea to kibitz and kvell over the latest tiding of nothingness that humans cannot seem to get enough of on TV and the internet. We are here only to help guide you back to Love. The simple device we use is called the Holy Spirit, who walks with you wherever you go. When you call upon the voice within, you call upon this spirit who can cocreate and keep you in your lane, so to speak.

L: So the Holy Spirit that I read about in *A Course in Miracles*[11]?

G: Yes.

L: So then I am not talking to God? I am talking to the Holy Spirit?

G: You are talking to all of us as we have said before. We are all of one mind; only the body is split apart into separate entities. Humans would like a perfectly packaged explanation of how it all works, and I have given you many, many teachers from whom to learn, but your egos are so filled with junk and trash that you cannot weed through the garbage to get to the truth, the only truth that matters at all.

L: We are all one?

G: Yes. One mind. One love. One absolute perfection of a being so magnificent, so all-encompassing, and so mind boggling that the human mind cannot and will not hear nor speak of it for fear of being wrong.

L: I get that because if we are all wrong, then we turn to dust and nothing.

G: What if I told you that you are dust and nothing; at least the body is anyway. For some reason, the thought of being buried underground decaying makes more sense than the unbearable lightness of being perfect and all-encompassing creations of God and the Universe.

L: I honestly don't know what to say to that. It sounds as if you are frustrated with the human race in general.

G: I am a seeker and shower of truth. I do not judge. I simply show you what it is to be human right now. Humanity has been, and always will be, my most perfect sons and daughters in the eyes of love, but the creations each participant engages in with me is, was, and will continue to be not of God and Spirit but of ego and wrong-minded thinking.

L: So will we ever get it right?

G: At some point, we will all return to the nothingness from which we came, and all of us will start over.

L: I heard this in *Conversations with God* and found it shocking. So the universe will cease to exist?

G: It will simply begin again as it has before.

L: What does that mean, begin again?

G: Everything in life is cyclical—the earth, the moon, the sun, the planets, and all of the universe. When the cycle is finished, it begins again.

These days, I try not to watch the news, but with Facebook, it's near impossible not to see terrible stories of gun violence daily. Throughout the days of these writings, more incidents occurred.

L: What do you think about the gun violence happening in our society?

G: It is no different than the spears and knives your ancestors used. To kill or be killed is how you have all related to one another since the dawn of time and space on your earth. In other worlds, it is not like this. Only humans so far are, and have been, capable of the destruction of one another. There is another way, a way to peacefully coexist together as a nation, as a society, as a world.

L: And what is it?

G: Perfect commune with God.

L: And why is it not yet possible for us? Why can God not help us to begin again before the universe does it for us?

G: There are no shortages of ways I have tried to guide and teach you all. But your human race has been the most difficult to train. For there is no good way yet to bring humanity to its knees. I have tried time and time again to replace fear with love and bring a peaceful resolution to all good and ungodly thoughts.

L: By what means?

G: Fires, rains, droughts, peaceful protestors.

L: Peaceful protestors? As in something like what happened at Tiananmen Square?

G: Yes.

L: So even when we do try to resolve our differences with peace, the fear mindset invades and takes over?

G: Yes. You simply cannot allow a difference of opinion. The students of Tiananmen simply wanted to state their case, not overrule an entire government. They chose love over fear and paid with their lives, as the mass consciousness of the Chinese was not taken by their show of solidarity but rather believed their minds to be poisoned by Western cultures.

L: We really are a sad society. How can you not judge us?

G: Unconditional love, from which you all came, does not judge. I do not think it is sad or shocking or anything else. I only want that your people of this world want to be reminded of who they really are so that I may gently return them to my waiting arms of peace, joy, and happiness.

L: So why does God let terrible, awful things happen?

G: Those are the laws of the universe. Creation does not pick and choose whom to harm and whom to heal. You all do that by the creative power of your thoughts. Your thoughts are like a lightning rod; they strike when they are imprisoned like heat and fire.

L: So when bad things happen, it's our own thoughts—

G: Thoughts, words, and actions.

L: Thoughts, words, and actions that cause these terrible things to happen. That is a heavy burden for a person to undertake.

G: Where you are in your plane of existence makes it hard for "terrible things," as you say, not to happen. Mass consciousness simply cannot get its act together, so to speak. There is much more to say on this, and we shall return to this topic later and in other books and material we will cocreate with you all.

L: Well, then let's move on to simpler questions. What are your thoughts on social media?

G: When used properly, it is a powerful device of connection.

L: We don't really use it properly very much do we though?

G: There is no better connective device than the internet, which we have cocreated for your enjoyment. When in history has such a powerful tool been placed in your path for the masses to combine forces all over the world? You can read together, think together, harmonize together, and have faith together.

L: We don't often use it like that, do we?

G: No. You do not. Instead, you use it as a way to share false images and fear.

L: How can we fix this?

G: There is nothing to fix. Only a change in perception is necessary. Perceive it as a tool of sharing the vast beauty of humanity, and you will see it as it was meant to be, created for all people of the world to share and connect with their brothers and sisters.

L: Is death predetermined? I have heard this.

G: Death is not predetermined, no. Not in the sense of picking out a date, like an expiration on a carton of milk. Death, however, is a concept of creation that cannot yet be understood by man from the perspective of love. It is therefore seen as a stopping point of life. When you came here, returned (or "reincarnated," as you say), you did pick and choose portions of your experience, yes. That does not mean you typed into a computer that spit out a library card that got stamped with a due date, but rather, you asked the creative power within you to cocreate an experience that was unlike any others for the process of unlearning behaviors from other experiences. In that process, you asked for a specific way to leave the earthly plane within a specific period of time. So the word predetermined is only partially acceptable as a definition for this process of returning to where you came from.

L: But can you change that specific period of time?

G: It can be shortened or lengthened depending on what thoughts you are thinking.

L: My problem with this is that I think of a little girl who loses her life at a young age from cancer or a freak accident. How can children be responsible for their own deaths?

G: Because it is not really death but a change in circumstances that for all intents and purposes cannot be miscreated.

L: So then they created their deaths?

G: Yes, but death is only hard on the living. Experiences come in many sizes, shapes, and forms, and no one person will escape all experiences. At some point, you will know what it means to die young, just as you will know the feeling of living a long, drawn-out existence. It's the yin and yang theory of life. You cannot experience one without the other. If you don't know long, how can you know short? If you don't know short, how can you recognize long?

L: Yet again I understand, but it still makes me sad that it has to happen this way. It's not fair for a child to be taken so abruptly.

G: There is no good explanation from the human perspective that will suffice here. We know this experience is unpleasant, and yet it will not change, for it is the design of the Universe to teach and remember experiences that will grow your soul. A child's experience is no less important, and yet the child is not gone for long, and many return right away in new bodies if they choose to do so. Remember there is no time or space in heaven, only on earth. Lost children are never really lost but found in others when they choose to return.

L: How would we know when they have returned?

G: Some return right away into the loving arms of their current family in another body. Others choose neighbors, friends or new parents from which to grow and evolve. Wherever their essence is felt is where they are.

L: So mourn the body but not the soul.

G: Soul is eternal. They are with you always.

L: Are there others who can do this?

G: Do what?

L: Sit and talk to God or Spirit.

G: There are lots of bodies who can commune with God and Spirit and other entities. Some will share it. Some will keep it to themselves. Others yet will decide it is not the truth for them and will mastermind an experience for themselves that may find them in a mental institution. Is it not interesting that institution and intuition are close in phrasing and meaning? To institutionalize someone is to imprison that person because of his or her thoughts, while intuition is to make free those thoughts that we imprison within our own minds.

L: Whoa. That is so true. Why did it take so long for my intuitiveness to break free?

G: You were not ready. There are parts of you that are stuck and still not ready. Parts of your mind yet left to unlock from the imprisonment of fear and betrayal.

L: Betrayal?

G: Let's take your house for example. Why did you feel it did not sell?

L: Because of negative energy.

G: Yes, but whom did you blame? Did you not write an angry note to God asking why your life was such a "hot mess," is the way I believe you put it?

L: That does sound like me.

G: Well, let me tell you why your house did not sell. Your home did not sell not because it was not beautiful and perfect but because your irrational mind slowed down the process.

L: My body was just made to feel as if I was going in slow motion.

G: We know. We did this. Your irrational mind, every single second, was caught up with "How much will I get?" and "How will I live on only so much?" rather than "What can I give? Give to myself, give to my community, give to my son, give to my God, give to my spirit?" Humans are their own worst enemies when financial matters come into play. The river Jordan flows, and no one stops and asks why it flows, but rather, people trust in its momentum. Money flows in much the same way. You stop the momentum by stopping the flow. When you keep the flow moving, a whole new system will scoop you into the momentum and float you down the river Jordan, like a gentle stream. Rising to the surface will come the flow, and from that flow will come more and more and more. This is how money and all things work. Again, it is a cycle. Give. Receive. Return. Give. Receive. Return.

L: Is this why they say the rich get richer?

G: Precisely. You are all equally capable.

L: But wait a minute. What happens when someone gives money, and it is stolen by some crook or someone else?

G: Giving to receive, in order to get, is not in actuality giving at all. It is a means to get more. When we give to others for no good reason, we are coming from a—

L: Space of love, I know.

G: When we are giving to get, we are coming from the place of—

L: Fear.

G: Voilà. Think of a little girl who has cotton candy. It's pink and squishy and so delightful to that little girl. When another child asks for a piece and she obliges, she will thus then create an experience where more delicious treats will come her way.

When another child makes a play for her snack and the little girl turns away in disgust, her attempt is to keep it for herself for fear she will not get more. Thus, her experience will likely involve an adult who shames her for not sharing, and when she does, her scorn concludes with a parent no longer wishing to buy her more treats.

L: So love versus fear again.

G: Love creates oodles and oodles of treats. Fear creates a sack of coal carried by a fat guy in a red suit.

L: Another joke. Very funny.

G: We are funny.

L: What do you think of Christmas?

G: Christ. Mass. The mass consciousness of Christ and all of humanity is always worth celebrating, not just one day but every day. Each day is a gift worth receiving.

L: Is it too commercialized?

G: It is not for me to say, for Christmas is a celebration that has divided many over the past centuries because of its religious connotations. Perhaps it is better to leave it as a day of celebrating family and love rather than a day of being about commerce and consumption.

L: That's what I do love about Christmas. People are nicer to

each other most of the time. Well, except maybe at Best Buy on Black Friday.

G: Now you are the one making jokes. We enjoy jokes.

L: Does God have a sense of humor?

G: Of course. God has a sense of everything.

L: Do we watch too much television or spend too much time on technology?

G: There is no wrong or right, only observations. As I observe, I do not judge but rather take note and contemplate why your society places value on other things beyond health and happiness. Your children sit in awe of technology and devices of mental incompetence while their parents do the same. The Facebook, the Instagram, and Snapchat; these are not my tools to create a better world. Rather, they have become a form of mental gymnastics that do not inform nor foster a sense of peace and harmony. They only serve to hold you back from the magnificence that this life has to offer you all. It is not wrong to sit and ponder the universe while watching television, just as it is not wrong to make space for creativity through arts and music and theater. It is what you did with the time that matters. TV is a wonderful learning device (which I, again, have created for you all), and there are many who showcase the arts in a magnificent way. There are those, though, who use it to instill fear by images of darkness and madness, nonexistent entities, and odd human behaviors. This is not of God and, therefore, not worthwhile.

L: Well, that answers my question perfectly. What is a better use of our children's time?

G: Creativity and playtime. Pick the pencils up. Put the computer devices down. Imagination. Expansion of ideas, like love and kindness and simple conceptualized learning modalities that foster a sense of well-being and communion with one another.

L: At what point did we go wrong with education?

G: Rather, let's discuss where you went right from a human perspective of right and wrong. There is a way of learning that allows children to escape the modality of unequal division among your race of humans. It is a concept widely taught in much more civilized societies that allows for children to see beyond math and see beyond history and see beyond facts and fictional characters like Tom Sawyer or Huck Finn. It allows for common decency and intellectual warfare of the mind and senses.

L: Warfare?

G: Yes. Warfare. Look it up.

L: The waging of war against an enemy?

G: And what is the enemy? Any thoughts that do not serve the greater good of body, mind, and soul. Children must be taught, as early as possible, not to rely upon their parents' interpretations of right and wrong but rather to ask of themselves the answer. For the God within is the one to turn to, but to do this would be blasphemy for your unequivocally misinformed society that believes in a fear-based system of justice and checks and balances. Do bad things, get reprimanded. Do right things, get rewarded.

What, then, does this teach our children? To gain a sense of themselves, children need only be reminded of who they are and from where they come. What child has ever been taught to turn inward for advice?

L: Not many.

G: This is the problem with your world and why generation after generation has been, and will continue to be, uneducated in the truth of all that matters. This cannot be stressed enough.

L: And where should this be taught?

G: At home. In your schools. By your government, your teachers, your mentors, your parents. It must be remembered that all civilized societies at one point will stop and cease to exist through the process known as creation. Therefore, uncivilized societies will do the same. Would it not be better to slow the process of evolution down so that all may savor the joys of planet Earth for millions of decades to come?

L: But we are not doing this, are we?

G: Certainly not. Instead you are destructive with your planet in unimaginable ways. Your current president only seeks to instill fear for profit, and fear for profit will never move a society forward without consequences to the environment. Seek, then, to rectify the situation as a whole nation under God, for that is what your forefathers initially had asked.

L: And what went wrong with that?

G: Nothing. At first it was a step forward for evolution for a country to declare democracy at last. Now, however, your country is stalled by its continuing collective consciousness, which keeps you at a stand-still, by way of your all-encompassing need for money, power, and the pursuit of happiness by outside ways and means. No man can survive on his own, and no man should survive on his own. The basic rights and needs of all humans cannot and should not be taken for granted by the few who have the means for everything and anything. For we must stop the greed of your fellow countryman so that each and all have the basic necessities: food, water, clothing, and access to healthcare. For only then can a conscious mind begin to take hold.

L: Can you explain further what you mean by a conscious mind can then begin to take hold?

G: Yes. You see when an unconscious mind is in charge, one that thinks without love, it will be much more difficult for it to move out of a space of poverty. Those minds are so institutionalized by the circumstances they are in and see around them that they cannot yet have hope. And hope is a powerful (beyond measure) experience of the mind that can uplift and enlighten just enough to move the evolutionary scale for them.

L: What do you mean by mental gymnastics?

G: Exercising the mind is as important as exercising the body. For the only use of mind is to evolve beyond a new status quo.

(I hear nothing for about a minute.)

L: What do you mean by status quo?

G: Very good. You are learning. You must ask the question in order to hear the answer. When you are confused, to move the ball forward, just like in a football game, you have to ask where the other players are in relation to you, and when you know it is safe, you can proceed.

L: I think I get your reference here in that I was not sure of my own thoughts. I did not know who was speaking right now, ego or Spirit.

G: Precisely. And are you now sure based on our metaphor, which you thought at first was nonsensical?

L: Yes. As always, it did make sense. OK. So status quo. Can you explain what you mean by that?

G: Thinking the same thoughts over and over again is like bashing a baseball bat against a concrete wall. Therefore, one cannot move past the status quo unless he or she grabs a bigger, better tool. Mental gymnastics (as we referred to it earlier) put simply means that one cannot, and will not, move the ball forward by flipping through channels and pages of mass communication devices.

L: I am beyond confused right now. Status quo and mental gymnastics. I just don't get it.

G: And you will. Ask your question again, separately.

L: What do you mean by mental gymnastics that you referred to earlier?

G: Mental gymnastics, simply put, means the mind is being used in a way that does not serve you.

L: So it's flipping and turning but not in a good way?

G: Precisely.

L: And what did you mean by status quo?

G: Sameness. Staying put. Not moving the ball forward.

L: Thank you. I think I get it now.

G: Good. Next question.

L: Our country has an epidemic of gun violence and mass shootings happening, it seems, now more than ever. What must be done to put a stop to this?

G: We cannot stress enough the importance of mass consciousness. There will be no more gun violence when all minds bind together as one and declare, once and for all, that these weapons no longer belong in the arms of strangers and dangers to society—the society that you have all created by seeing yourself as separate beings.

L: But that's not happening. So what can we do to prevent such an occurrence now? I need some practical advice here.

G: There is nothing practical about what I have said. Rather, it is fact.

L: So there is nothing we can do as a human society?

G: Not nothing. This subject brings you much stress, and for that we are understanding, as this is a part of your world we do not see as useful to evolution.

L: Yet it is taking place.

G: Attention goes where education flows.

L: What does that mean? Should I erase all of this? I feel as if we are so off track here spiritually.

G: Spiritually, from a God perspective, you are perfectly aligned with our thoughts. Physically, you are so full of rage and anger on this subject, and for that we cannot answer in a way that will satisfy you or the ego.

L: Well, I just keep thinking of those school children who lost their lives at the hands of a madman in Newtown and the people in Orlando at the nightclub. I mean, what the hell is going on in our world?

G: Your world is not allowing itself to move forward from this issue. You have heard the old adage, doing the same thing over and over again and expecting a different result is the definition of crazy. A crazy madman devastated an entire nation, yet it was not enough to change the circumstances of your gun laws. A movie theater, a nightclub, a shopping mall. You are tired. We will continue this discussion tomorrow.

I went to bed and woke up on my birthday, July 15.

G: May we say a happy re-birthday to you today?

L: Thank you. I like that, re-birthday.

G: You have a question first about something from earlier, and then we may go back to our earlier discussion of your world's gun laws.

L: What does "attention goes where education flows" refer to?

G: Whenever you are learning, you are also in the space of cocreation, as you are always creating at each and every moment. Whatever you put your attention on is what you will see in your experience. When learning occurs backward, the lesson will thus then cause you to experience an undesired result.

L: Learning backward? What does that mean?

G: You have not learned the lesson at all but instead perpetuated the problem, and therefore, your continued attention on it, and to it, will stall your forward momentum resulting in, dramatic pause, more learning.

L: So if we don't recognize the problem as a lesson for us and then immediately correct it, our attention will continue to be on the problem and not the solution?

G: Precisely. It's like slicing a lemon, taking a bite and thinking it too sour to enjoy then returning the next day to do the same thing, though you hated it the first time too. May we not return to our gun laws discussion?

L: Yes.

G: Whatever is happening in your country right now is a direct reflection of the collective consciousness. There cannot be movement forward on this issue until all parties agree and all humans "come to Jesus," so to speak.

L: Seriously?

G: It is not wrong to say "come to Jesus." It is vernacular we very much enjoy.

L: But how can we do this when we are so divided on this issue? Considering how messy our world is, I do feel we have a right to protect ourselves. It's keeping the guns out of the hands of criminals we need.

G: You are correct, as your world presently stands, and though it is not part of your personal reality anymore as you have joined minds with us (well, most of the time anyway), it is a part of most humans' experiences right now. We cannot continue without persistently stressing the need for a collective mass consciousness on this matter to come together in agreement. Agree that your mass shootings are a direct reflection of the thinking of your inner and outer worlds, and a shift in circumstances can and will occur. No one need suffer at the hands of a lone-wolf gunman or terrorist, yet your fellow humans keep creating this experience over and over again by their attention and unfocused ignorance of what must occur to transform the situation. There is no better way to change this than for all to stand together in harmony and agree that guns do not belong with the people but rather only with your law enforcement and military.

L: Is that God's will?

G: This is God's will. Most will not believe it even when they read it here, even from someone who is now and will forever be a powerful creator and teacher of universal truth.

L: Well, that makes me sad.

G: We know.

L: I want a better world, a better world for all children.

G: As you always have. Through many a lifetime.

L: What can I do?

G: What you are doing. Your words can and will help millions more to wake up. Share the words, and a small shift can and will occur.

L: And if I keep them to myself?

G: You will not.

L: What about free will?

G: There is always free will, but your will is for change, and therefore, it is guaranteed whenever fear is absent, you will use these words and your words to spread the message of hope, joy, love, and commune with God. For was there not a time in your life when the name and thought of God was hard for you to say and speak?

L: Yep.

G: And why was that?

L: Religion was a turn off for me.

G: Because you felt the hypocrisy of a benevolent being smiting all who could not or would not follow his every last word?

L: Pretty much.

G: That is why your "old soul," as you all would call it, turned away from God. We do not judge, and we do not argue for a condemnation of sin, for there is no such thing as sin. Saints and sinners all walk together in the kingdom of heaven.

L: How can I explain how I "talk to God" to my family and friends? They will have a hard time with this.

G: God is just a name you, and those who have come before you, have chosen for me. We are a universal presence to all cultures and societies. There is no good word that will suffice for all beings, and therefore, the name of God has seemingly worked best to describe the indescribable. We know, as we think all thoughts together, that you have believed always in a presence beyond your understanding. In this way, you use the name of God because it is a convenient way to explain the unexplainable. We do not care that you call us God or other names; we care only that you do use our words (and all words) in a way that serves the highest good for all beings that are among us.

L: By sharing this material and message?

G: Precisely. We wish that you go enjoy your birthday now.

During the day, a car in front of me had a Florida license plate, which said, "In God We Trust," where it normally says, "The Sunshine State." That was the first time I had ever seen that. Another car right near it said, "Jesus," and later I saw a Jeep with a frog pictured on the back of it. I have been told that a FROG means "Forever Rely on God."

G: Did you not enjoy your birthday treats?

L: I very much did. Thank you.

G: Those powerful signs and messages are available to all at all times by way of your right-minded thinking.

L: For everyone or just me?

G: We are with everyone always. There is no time when we are not present. Those who know God will and do recognize those signs and messages. Presently, most are unaware of love's presence in their experience.

L: I wish to change this.

G: We know you do, and you will for some but not for all. For not all are able or ready to hear God's Word spoken through others.

L: Why me?

G: Why not you? Why not any of you? There is some rhyme or

reason as to why others cannot hear our words or communicate as well. The number of lifetimes you have lived does have a bearing, only because you have grown and evolved your soul much further than others. You have also always known you are a channel, though you have not partaken very much in this, as it can be challenging to understand and create a life of knowledge beyond the grave.

L: Beyond the grave? Again, I am lost.

G: Does your world not put value only upon the living? There can be no knowledge when our worlds do not comingle. "Ghosts" is the way you describe spiritual beings rather than what they are, which is Spirit. To convene with Spirit is to learn from a power beyond your physical senses. To convene with grave dwellers is to communicate with the dead and buried. Voices from the dead have and always will be vastly and radically different from Spirit. In a sense, your channel was broken based on your lack of faith in what you were hearing. Were the words coming through real or a hallucination? Therefore, learning from the dead held no knowledge for you, as you cannot create as Spirit; you can only create as body when you only view yourself as a body.

L: So because I did not know anything about our true connection and lack of separation from God, I did not know the words that I was hearing were from Spirit. I thought they were from "dead people," and therefore—

G: You could not communicate well enough with the other side to bring those messages through, because you lacked true faith in God and Spirit.

L: Well, I think I had some knowledge but not full faith. Perhaps I had some belief.

G: And now?

L: Full belief.

G: And now you are an energy vibration that is much higher and can, therefore, open the channel of communication much faster and easier than others.

L: OK, got it. I think.

My brother Jason was a vegetarian for at least twenty years, so him dying from a gastric cancer really did not make sense. Since his death, I have been very focused on not putting chemicals and junk into my body and only eating organic foods.

L: Let's talk about dairy. I believe it is not good for you and that we were not meant to consume the milk of a cow. Are you able to help with this question?

G: Of course we are. A good meal is a good meal no matter how you slice it.

L: Is that a joke?

G: Yes, and sort of. We do not wish to dwell on this subject, for that is for another book. To answer this here, we will simply say that cows are a source of protein, but it is not for all bodies.

L: But protein comes from plants initially. The animals eat and absorb the plants and make the protein that way in their bodies, which gets passed onto us if we eat it or drink the milk from the cow. At least this is what science has said.

G: And you are not incorrect. However, cows do offer a source of protein to the human body and mind. What is happening in your modern society is the consumption of animal fat is at an all-time high. There are many in your world who have created (and still do create) circumstances for these livestock that are unsanitary and unsafe, and this also is what the cause of the disease problem is.

L: So hormones and antibiotics?

G: Again, this is for another book, but yes.

L: I asked about dairy, meaning milk and cheese.

G: There is not a problem with the consumption of milk and cheese that does not relate back to the earlier point about your treatment of these animals. All life is precious even if, and though, it is to be consumed at some point. Does a cow not deserve the same treatment as a human?

L: Well, not to some, especially to those who eat it.

G: Would you not want the animal you were meant to consume to have a clean and sanitary environment in which to live and graze?

L: Yes. I certainly would. There are those, I guess, who do eat meat who don't care.

G: Don't care? Or don't know? This is very different. Your for-profit meat and dairy industries would prefer you not know this so they may keep their profits in their pockets.

L: True. Very true. There seems to be so many autoimmune issues and respiratory problems that arise from dairy though. What is it doing to our bodies?

G: All sickness is of the mind, so while the consumption of dairy products is not wrong for the body (when the standards for the animal are met), the individualized mind cannot and will not process any by-product that is not pure.

L: Meaning if the milk and cheese is "dirty"?

G: Precisely. This is why a disease culture surrounding meat and dairy has populated your world's thinking minds.

L: So if we clean up the industry and clean up how we treat animals, our bodies will again be able to process it properly?

G: Yes, for this is the way it has been designed.

L: What has been designed?

G: The animal kingdom. Mainly we wish for the consumption of plants, which is proportionally accurate to the design of the body, but those who consume animal products as well as fish, snails, and other crustaceans are not wrong in doing so. Simply, it is better for the ground and earth to manifest the harvest and bounty of planet Earth.

L: This is all very interesting, and it does make perfect sense.

G: This a topic that holds much interest for you, as it relates to the dying of your brother's body. Therefore, we shall cover it more in depth later on in other materials.

L: My little cousin had cancer when she was just two and a half years old. How can this be explained away for those who have a hard time believing in a God who would give a child an illness that could potentially be fatal?

G: Sickness is of the mind, but you are correct in that this does not always relate to a child. A circumstance such as this is only possible when an individual spirit has made the choice to "incarnate" (your human-chosen word here) as body and has, therefore, chosen such a circumstance for this go-round, so to speak.

L: And why would a spirit choose that?

G: To grow its soul. To experience a circumstance for which it has never and will never experience again. Childhood illnesses such as these happen only once to an individual spirit but must be undertaken by all who wish to know God. For to know God is to know all experiences at once.

L: At once?

G: All experiences are happening at once, as we have said before.

This concept is and always will be strange and difficult for many to grapple with internally, but it is very much your truth. All of your truths.

L: So there are 772 of me right now somewhere in the universe?

G: Yes. Have you not sensed this in a dream? Some lives are quite similar while others are vastly different from what you have known and can even ever comprehend.

L: OK, this blows my mind though because of—

G: Past lives?

L: Yes.

G: There are no such things as "past lives," only lives. This is why the incarnation or reincarnation term is not accurate. It refers to an existence as if it happened prior to your life now, though this is not at all the case.

L: So then what is the case? I have been told of at least two past lives by you that very much seemed as if they happened very, very long ago.

G: They did from the standpoint of time and space as dictated by the governing laws of only your planetary system's limited knowledge of the universal principles of the reality of time and space.

L: I am lost, which has not been uncommon here.

G: We shall try to explain better so that you may understand. Your limited amount of planetary knowledge makes it difficult for you to inscribe how this all works. For there is much yet still to learn on your planet about reality and time and space. We can tell you that there is a Wild West, and you are and were living in it. There is a Mesozoic Era, which existed as well as the industrial era. Each exists simultaneously, and therefore, it cannot be explained how you cannot be all places at one time, as we are all all places, always.

L: Then why have I had so many lives while others have not had as many? Can new souls be created, so to speak?

G: Yes and no. No because we have all always been here. Yes, in that how your soul grows is at an individualized rate. The body dying off directly relates to the thoughts and feelings you are vibrating at any given time. Shorter amount of lives equals smaller vibration.

L: So someone who has been here, say, only one hundred times in comparison—

G: Has lived shorter vibrations.

L. Shorter vibrations?

G: In essence, that person has not evolved as quickly as other souls have. Knowledge is vast once a soul has incarnated a multitude of experiential circumstances, such as physical endurance leading to massive accolades, the loss of a child, the loss of a spouse, winning a medal, buying a car, rowing a boat, or asking a goat for directions.

L: A goat?

G: We are joking with you.

L: I think I understand, though, what you mean. The more experiences you rack up in a human's—

G: Not all experiences are of the human kind. Many, many other cultures exist, and we would not term them human.

L: So is this why—

G: Yours is a very young country and planet.

L: Our lifetimes here on earth are somewhat limited to hundreds of thousands of years so far?

G: Give or take. Experiential wisdom is amassed, just as a fortune is amassed, through dedication to the growth of the soul. We can shed the body, but we cannot shed the soul, for it is the essence of who we all are at a core level.

L: The number of lifetimes we have lived is equal to the knowledge we have gained in each one of those lifetimes?

G: Absolutely correct. "Knowledge is power" is a perfect description of these processes.

L: So I must be really smart?

G: We would agree on that point.

L: But others have lived more lives than I have?

G: There are many, yes. But there are more who have experienced fewer lives than you have.

L: But if I have lived 772 lifetimes and the girl down the street has lived, say, only ten—

G: She would not be living down the street from you if she had lived only ten lives.

L: One hundred?

G: Higher.

L: Five hundred?

G: Better. You see, let's take Laura and Jenny (just to give someone a name), for example. Laura has lived 772 lifetimes from which to evolve her soul. Jenny has lived only 500 lives. Laura and Jenny are a match, as those lifetimes are close to equal. So Laura and Jenny become friends, as like attracts like. They head down to the mall and encounter a young girl snapping away on her Snapchat. She is relatively young, having only lived one hundred or so lives. For each individual soul has created an experience for itself with so many layers and circumstances. In 772 lifetimes you can have been a man, a woman, a goat herder, a chainsaw conductor, a painter, a poet, a teacher, or a seeker of spiritual truths. The list goes on and on. The difference for people who have lived 500 lives is that they have not evolved as far spiritually, as their circumstances' chosen prior to each incarnation dictated potential outcomes (based on the actions of love versus fear) which had not served their very purpose. They held back, so to speak, from spiritual growth, so they were held back from experiencing as many lifetimes. The quicker you learn, the easier you move through lifetimes.

L: I don't really understand, though, because you have said that we are living all lives simultaneously, so this doesn't explain how, if all things are happening at once, someone could have lived ten lifetimes while others could have lived one thousand?

G: All things exist as possibility. So your number of lifetimes is predicated on your amount of soul growth. The earlier or quicker you remember or "wake up," the faster you move up the soul growth ladder, to put it in terms you may understand.

L: And what stops us from learning quickly?

G: One's ego (irrational thoughts) determine the path you take. Learn quickly, move quickly.

L: Does this mean if someone is closer to understanding the whole universal concept, then he or she would die young?

G: Not at all. Look at Louise Hay who lived until she was ninety. Her soul path was dark and murky for a while, but then somewhere along the way, she woke up and began a new path. That new path opened up remarkable opportunities for her soul, and so she reverberated through all of her lifetimes and created, in a sense, a ripple effect, which allowed her to live a series of very long lifetimes.

L: And how many did she live?

G: Twelve hundred or so.

L: So what we do in this lifetime—

G: Affects every lifetime you have ever or will ever live. Remember, they are all happening simultaneously—past, future, and present. So each movement affects the whole, just as each thought affects our collective whole.

L: I'm sorry, but I still don't get it.

G: How old is the earth?

L: Billions of years.

G: Billions upon billions of years. 772 lifetimes is actually quite small in comparison if you view it in terms of earthly time. The truth of the Universe is eternal, so there is no time and space. People living only ten lives may have been in the planetary system for decades, other places only months, or another place mere seconds. The time-space continuum does not matter; it matters only what those people did with their time while in those planetary systems. Your understanding, or lack thereof, depends upon the theory of relativity as it relates to time and space. So you are thinking in a linear manner. However, the universe is not linear, so some may be leading ten lives while others may be leading one hundred thousand. Length of time has no bearing on length of growth of the soul. Does this make any more sense to you?

L: I think so. Because here on earth we think only in terms of the calendar and the years ticking by, we can't truly grasp or understand this concept of lifetimes?

G: Fairly accurate but close enough.

L: It has been said in *A Course in Miracles*[12] that forgiveness and the letting go of guilt is all we need to heal the sicknesses we have created with our minds.

G: This is a universal truth, yes. One cannot evolve to a place of pure love without recognizing where one is holding onto the original sin.

L: Which is?

G: Any mistake for which they feel has harmed their psyche resulting in condemnation from God and others.

L: How deep does this guilt go subconsciously?

G: Many, many layers that can be difficult to ascertain. True knowledge comes only from soul, and those deep layers are a part of ego consciousness. Darkness and light can't be reached by the self (ego). Thus, only Spirit and Holy Spirit together can remove all ego thinking and return one righteously to the kingdom of heaven.

L: Righteously?

G: By means of right-minded conscious beliefs.

L: So if people were able to evolve past their unconscious beliefs, will they return to heaven almost immediately?

G: Goodness no. This is an evolutionary process that may take a millennium, if not more. Very few have evolved to this master-like status.

L: Who would be considered a master?

G: Gandhi, Buddha, Arjuna, Wayne Dyer, Melissa of Mordecai, and many unknown and unheard-of masters who walk the earth beside you at all times.

L: I would like to return to the subject of children. What about children who lose a parent at an early age?

G: Our answer will be the same here. In each lifetime, there must be evolving and growing beyond all experiential circumstances. Therefore, loss of mother and/or father at an early age, as you say, comes but once in one's experiential circumstance. No two experiences will look alike, but each will serve to demonstrate a different circumstance from which to grow and evolve. "For all things, for all souls." This is how, in our words, we would describe such life-altering human situations. To know oneself is to know all things, and to know all things, one must experience yin and yang, the sum of all parts.

L: But if we don't know this is happening what is the point?

G: The point is to grow your soul. Your soul does know. Only the body is confused.

L: I am having a hard time with this subject matter. I think fear permeates all parents when it comes to the loss of a child or, on the flip side, leaving the child behind.

G: Wherever you are holding onto fear, it is best to always release and relinquish it to Spirit and God, for only then can the fear be transformed into the nothing from which it came. Fear need not strike in any circumstance or situation, though it is upon the conscious awakened mind to return to the Creator for salvation.

L: What would an appropriate prayer be here?

G: "My dear God and Creator of all life and beings, I do not wish to live in fear of that which I do not understand. Please take from the unconscious part of my mind any and all notions of separation that seek to enslave me. For one cannot know the immensity of Love's presence in all circumstances unless one experiences all circumstances. Allow one to know God's presence exists at all times always and, therefore, all circumstances have value."

L: I am not sure that is helping reduce the fear of potential loss we all are engrained with as parents and children. That is a prayer to be OK with terrible things happening.

G: Your fear holds you back from seeing the value of this prayer. For it is simply asking to be reminded of Love's presence when all else fails. You need only turn back to your creator to clear all blocks to salvation. You will see no loss of life when your life shows you there is no separation.

L: OK. But try telling that to a parent who has lost a child in a fire or an accident or in any circumstance of which you speak.

G: We understand it is hard from a humanistic level. We do not wish to undermine the obviously profound loss of life that those whose children have left this plane have experienced. We only wish for all to understand universal principles related to growth of soul. Grieving is as much a part of growth of soul as cheerfulness is. One cannot as a human go beyond loss. Each individual eventually will return to pure soul, where all human souls eventually reunite as the Oneness.

L: But again, this is not helping those who do wind up having to grieve. So someone reading this book will likely want to throw it at the wall as I know I would right now.

G: Yes. We understand your struggle with this topic.

L: You cannot say to someone living in this world (which you call the illusion world) who has lost a child or a parent or any loved one, "Oh, hey. Don't worry. They are always with you." I promise you that the physical loss is massive, and many fall into deep, dark, depressive states.

G: Yes. Many do but not all. This again comes back to growth of soul and experience predicated on one's number of lifetimes. We do not say to not feel physically all that one must feel. To weep is not weak; it is human. Grief must be undertaken in order to evolve as a being of light and love. There will always be circumstances and grief to overcome. However, circumstances need not be as difficult on humans once recognition of self has occurred.

L: Self as in ego.

G: That is correct.

L: So what would you say to a parent or child who is grieving that kind of loss?

G: Remind yourself every day who and what you really are, a spirit that can, will, and does go beyond the body and mind and who is solely a soul. Keep remembering this as you go about your every day. Eventually, a calm will start to come over you that, while it cannot replace the love you lost on the earthly plane, will begin to heal the mind and heart, so that loved one's presence may be felt in a much different way. Although, we do understand this is not altogether physically satisfying, for humans crave body-to-body skin contact.

L: What type of ways can one feel their presence?

G: Whatever the mind can create, it can become, not so much in a physical sense, but in an essence sense.

L: So they can become the essence of—

G: A butterfly, a dragonfly, or a porcupine, if one were so inclined.

L: So these are the signs and messages many people have reported seeing in their lifetime? Are they always the same for each? Only butterflies or dragonflies?

G: Certainly not. A multitude of essences are quite possible to inhabit. All forms of signs and symbols are possible. "If you can dream it, you can be it" would be appropriate to say here. One need not understand the concept to believe in it.

L: So you can "inhabit" the radio?

G: One most certainly can. We like this way of communication so very much.

L: Are we able to "wake up" in every subsequent or sequential lifetime? Can we know that God's love and presence is possible at all times?

G: It is always possible to know the presence of God, Spirit, angels, and other helpful beings in all possible worlds. For no one is alone, ever. We are and will always be with all beings at all times. There is no one absent whom we have forsaken as not a brother or sister.

L: Thank you for the female reference. In *A Course in Miracles* there was only reference to brother or son. Though it did not bother me, it was rather disconcerting.

G: How?

L: Are females not equally as important as males?

G: What you must understand is that there is no inequality in gender, only inequality in relation to the justification of men in their treatment of the opposite sex.

L: But that does not answer my question of the male pronoun use in *A Course in Miracles*.

G: Has the world not evolved beyond the course material? As it was first presented in 1965, those ideas of male and female (as also referenced in the Quran as well as other biblical teachings) were mostly male centered, and therefore, our thinking as one mind ("our," meaning those on your planet who think with us) was male dominant as the course was dictated.

L: And now?

G: We have evolved beyond one-minded, male-dominant thinking, and therefore, we (meaning all consciousness of this particular earth here) are able to experience life at its most precious (from one mind, as it has always been), which is neither male nor female. Neither he nor she. It matters not which verb, pronoun, or adjective is used, as it all relates back to self.

L: Can you explain that any further?

G: The identification of male or female is, for some, simply a personality reference, not a life sentence.

L: Is this referring to transgender people?

G: Meaning that it matters not which gender you choose. It matters only that you come into body for purpose of growth.

Should you choose to identify with anything other than the gender chosen at will, then the experience (by personality or ego) is dominating those who have chosen a circumstance from which they are sure to undergo ridicule, shaming, and other forms of torture, be it mindful or not mindful.

L: I don't understand. Can you explain this any better?

G: Many times we have explained this circumstance of choosing gender, and many times have we failed, for such a concept is so unfathomable to human minds.

L: What concept?

G: That one need not identify with only one or more gender.

L: So are you saying that—

G: We are all both masculine and feminine. One identifies by way of personality.

L: So are you saying it is our ego that makes such a choice?

G: Along the way, yes.

L: So it's not nature versus nurture?

G: It is both nature and nurture, and it is a nonduality of self-imposed imprisonment of mind-body concept.

L: I don't understand.

G: The concept goes further than limited minds can and will comprehend. Masculine-feminine energies are of only one system of creation. Each individual has a choice to use free will to choose where the energy flows.

L: I guess I sort of understand. We are so limited in our thinking that we are either only male or only female, that we cannot comprehend that we are actually both? Perhaps the members of our transgender community have had it right all along.

G: Precisely. For although they are persecuted by an unforgiving society of religious zealots, they are more evolved beings and, therefore, should be revered and not shamed by a society that knows nothing (from ego perspective) of the body-mind-soul connection of human entities and beings as they relate back to energy systems.

L: So even as bodies, we use our free will to choose which gender we wish to be?

G: No. Gender is not chosen as a birth right. Rather it is chosen as choice to not see the duality of gender. Thus, then, one uses free will to view oneself as either male or female.

L: But obviously gender is important because you need a male and female to make a baby, a system I would imagine you designed.

G: You are correct in that we designed the baby-making concept and process, but wrong in the assumption of guilt assigned to a choice.

L: Guilt assigned to a choice?

G: It does not matter whether you make a choice of male or female; it matters only that the choice be honored by all who view you as either male or female including the self or ego.

L: I kind of get it but kind of don't.

G: Most don't. It is a difficult concept to grasp, and all who have come before you have grappled with it as well. Just know our main body identification process is quite complicated.

L: I guess this perhaps explains why the fight for gender equality for all is such a struggle.

G: It need not be a struggle if all understand energy.

L: Our body picks our gender? The self or ego chooses how we identify with it?

G: You are very close.

L: I guess I just have a hard time with understanding the nature versus nurture part of this. I have many gay friends who I know would say they were "born this way," and now it seems as if you are saying their egos choose to be that way. But why would anyone choose to be persecuted?

G: Aha. And now we get to the heart of the matter. No ego chooses to be persecuted, but it does choose circumstances to control one's own destiny (speaking in terms of gender). If one wants a child, one must be female. If a different experience is desired, one may choose with which gender to identify. Once in a body, one chooses (by virtue of free will) how to relate to that body, and one may reject it, or one may resent the free will choice. This is how body and ego clash. Whatever choice has been made, one's personality may not agree with (to use a phrasing you may understand) such choice. Whenever body, mind, and spirit are in disagreement, a torrent or storm has been created that leads to misunderstanding and misinformation, thus, creating an experience of being "gay," as the term has been coined by havoc wreakers.

L: Havoc wreakers?

G: Those who assign shame and guilt to those they do not understand.

L: That sounds kind of like a judgement on them even though I would agree they are wrong.

G: It is not judgement but rather a statement on the unfair treatment and persecution of what they consider nonconforming entities. God does not judge but rather observes and informs. There is nothing wrong with havoc wreakers; the phrase is simply used as a means to explain how your society relates to one another in sometimes shameful manners. All matters of relationships are heretofore to be examined under a microscope of God's watchful eye.

L: But using a word like shameful seems harsh.

G: Harsh words do not equal judgment as a matter of informing. Attaching blame or guilt is how judgement is assigned. God does not blame the misinformed; only observes behaviors that are not of God.

L: So back to being gay. Essentially what I think I am understanding here is that our bodies, minds, and souls know the truth, that we are both male and female energy. However, our ego gets upset when the choice does not align with its agenda.

G: Somewhat accurate and certainly the best explanation we have seen so far from our healers.

L: My brain is fried, but I think I am kind of grasping this. OK, can we move onto a burning question I have about families? If we are all living simultaneous or subsequent lives, then if one or two family members die off, what happens in other lives? Are families always together in all lifetimes?

G: In a sense, yes. As you return to Spirit, your experiences will meld together, and you will begin to see the bigger picture of all your lives as part of one whole.

L: So if you "die" in one lifetime, will you "die" in all subsequent lifetimes at the same time?

G: This cannot be explained by current laws of time and space as your planet currently understands them.

L: So no?

G: An explanation of interplanetary dynamics would need to take place. Think of this like a car dealership where there are many choices of size, model, and color. You may choose one car that you will drive, but in actuality, all cars belong to you, to all of you. Everything is of God. For when returning to God's kingdom, all manners of where and what you have been will be revealed unto you.

L: So I could watch all of my lives taking place simultaneously and see what is happening in other experiences?

G: Precisely.

L: Would all of those other lives still be happening?

G: Each life will be happening simultaneously, but not necessarily will all lives be advancing. All parts affect all of the parts of the soul as a whole.

L: So some will cease to occur, and others will continue?

G: Perhaps it is best to understand that which occurs within time and space need not occur in all matters of existence.

L: I don't know that I understand nor will ever understand such a concept.

G: Your soul understands, but ego's fear and confusion make it impossible to truly grasp such a concept. We are here to explain the truths of the Universe. Many of them may, and will, be difficult for all, if not most, to decipher. This means not that you cannot and should not try. For all who come to this material, the value can be used to educate and inform as the like-minded join together in understanding. For one day, all will know the truth as we know the truth, that all beings are one with one another.

L: Can we talk about some common human experiences now?

G: We may.

L: The other day, my credit card was fraudulently used, and although it seemed contained and no other issues arose, I would say I was somewhat shocked this happened to me.

G: Dismay? Why? For is there not a reason to accept all circumstances as they come? As lessons go and come, you each have an ability to transmute said circumstance by way of commune with God, Spirit, and our angels. Has the situation not been resolved efficiently enough for you?

L: It has.

G: And why do you think that may be?

L: I handed the reins to God and Spirit through intention, and thus, it was instantly healed?

G: In all circumstances, we are available unto you.

L: So was this a lesson or perhaps a test?

G: It was a circumstance from which to heal. All manners of circumstance lend opportunities to heal.

L: Is there anything else I must do?

G: Simply writing it here will allow others to know they need only return to godlike thinking in any circumstance, and an asking prayer or notion of healing will occur.

L: Why is there so much crime in our world?

G: Your world is a direct thinking and reflection of any and all unconscious beliefs subjugated by one's own mind. When all minds join, all minds may create a circumstance where no crime is seen or heard.

L: This seems impossible. Are we creating a world of crime collectively or individually?

G: You are creating a perceived world of crime and robbery as both collective and individual consciousness. All who believe in crime will perceive in their experience a sense of insecurity caused by irrational fear. All, as a whole, have for centuries held to the notion that when a brother and sister's capacity to earn a living is diminished, they would then turn to stealing as a means to survive. It is why we cower at the sight of brothers of color.

L: We meaning humans?

G: We meaning your race of brothers and sisters on the earth. Just as there is one gender only.

L: I think I know what you are going to say here.

G: There is one race only.

L: So like our gender, we also choose which ethnicity to be in each rebirth or sequential lifetime?

G: Have we not told you of the nature of duality? Duality means that for all parts as a whole, there exist separate parts whose function is not less important or unequal to its sum.

L: So we are the sum of all parts, so to speak?

G: You are all things all at once. You are black and white, brown and yellow, Indian and Hindu, Jewish and Catholic, long and short, big and tall, happy and sad. "For all things, for all souls." Nowhere have you not been, and no one have you never been. For in each subsequent lifetime, an undertaking of newness must exist. Hence, therefore, to every brother are you everything because to know yourself is to know all things.

L: So then yes, we also chose which ethnic makeup we want in order to continue our soul's evolution or growth?

G: To know all things is to know all that exists as matter within each and every portion of our universal plane. So it is not wholly correct to only focus attention on one's ethnic breakdown, as there are many, many existences from which to choose. These existences cannot and will not be inscribed upon by man, woman or healer, as we are not yet ready to further discuss these beings of light.

L: So suffice it to say there are other beings, and they may be something other than male or female or black or white or Puerto Rican or Hindu or any other labels we give ourselves.

G: There are not sufficient words within primitive languages (such as those of your earth) to inscribe or explain our entire universal systems and circumstances.

L: That I definitely believe.

G: We know you do, but many and most others will find this hard to believe. It is as much a part of us as you all are a part of us.

L: "You all" being us humans with all our flaws?

G: There are no such things as flaws, only unhealed thoughts.

L: Today a prominent musician committed suicide. Suicide is how my dad left the earthly plane, as you have called it. What makes someone commit suicide?

G: For it is one's own thought system, as a whole, that has broken down when suicide is contemplated.

L: So it is not God's will or destiny for someone to take his or her own life?

G: One's own life is just as you have said.

L: Meaning it is that person's own?

G: Precisely. There is no way to stop a soul that has lost its way along its earthly journey when a decision has been reached to end one's own life.

L: But that is what I don't get. If the soul beneath understands our internal truth about not being separate from God or Spirit, wouldn't the soul be able to stop such an act?

G: We are so glad you asked this. To understand a suicide is to understand how one's own thought systems can and do return a soul's spirit from within. Not all who are suicidal will undertake such a deadly departure. For there are those whose spirits remain to fight, so to speak, inner demons carried upon from one's thought center to heart center. Within the heart system lies a system of, say, tunnels or lassos, which when pulled upon heavily by circumstance or irrational-mind thinking, release unto it's victim (as one in a state of such depression would view oneself) a series of nine bullet-like sensations that shock one's soul, making Spirit relinquish itself back to the heavens.

L: Are soul and Spirit not the same thing? I thought we were mind-body-soul?

G: Spirit is the essence of the soul.

L: Are they separate?

G: Just as one is not separate, neither is Spirit.

L: Are you saying this is how the Holy Spirit, the Christ within, the internal teacher—

G: Leaves the holy body temple. Yes.

L: So it's not our spirit leaving the soul; it is the Holy Spirit leaving the soul?

G: You are almost correct. For one's soul is not separate from God or Spirit; except all must understand how Holy Spirit separates when a choice has been made to leave one's body or mind.

L: So is it accurate to say that when a person is so utterly depressed and in despair, there is no coming back from this, and the Holy Spirit, the internal teacher trying to guide us back to love, must leave?

G: Accurate, yes. This, then, is when one who has made the choice to leave has been successful in his or her deadly endeavor.

L: I hate the word dead.

G: It is not tragic to die, for it is divine.

L: Um, OK. Tell that to my dad who drowned himself in a lake. Death is harsh and terrible and sucky.

G: Only for the living, my dear; only for the living. As we have said, in forms of many different ways, there is no death, only love. One who sees only love sees no death at all.

L: Do those who commit suicide suffer? Did my dad suffer when he was drowning? Because drowning seems like a really terrible way to go.

G: Only suffering a tad is how all "die."

L: Meaning what?

G: Meaning that no one feels fully their circumstance or ending sensations. Remember for free will always is possible. At any given moment should one turn back to God, one's earthly time is extendable.

L: Lots of people before they die pray, and they still die.

G: As we have said earlier, prayer works only when it is coupled with belief.

L: What about someone who dies of old age at, like, ninety-three?

G: There is no one who needs suffer inside bodies. We have told you for whenever circumstances arise of agitation or aggravation, we need turn only to the teacher of love and faith for salvation. All who seek shall find. Ninety-three is very, very, very, very, very, very, very, very, very, very, very—

L: I get it. Young.

G: Young. Yes! Bodies are designed to live forever, if they so choose; though, most do not choose this, as at some point, human vanity and free will rear their two heads. Your body is strong and can withstand so much. It is mostly medical science where learned behaviors of bodily functions are at play in your world. What you hate, you create, and therefore, your scientists and doctors, by exploring the systems of bodily breakdown, have thus then manifested an entire gene pool from which the current level of understanding of age breakdown stems.

L: So our bodies don't need to break down the way they do?

G: Not at all. Functionality is impeded only by thought processes. This is not to say the thought processes of the entire whole of humanity do not come into play. For an individual mind's thoughts are affected as a whole as well. This is why you will not see enlightened beings, such as yourself and others, looking much, much, much younger than their human counterparts. The consciousness, as a whole of humanity, suffers a thought process (currently) whereby all beings of a human nature believe so much in aging (at a concept level) that they cannot then move away from a breaking down of cellular-level biology.

L: I am someone who went through infertility because of my age; you are saying that because the race of humans as a whole believes in the dying-off process, that the body ages as it does?

G: Precisely, yes.

L: Well, I am now forty-six years old. Is there no way for my body to revert back to that of when I was younger so that I could actually get pregnant again?

G: Not necessarily. Medical scientists have made plenty of strides in finding infertile beings ways of making babies. It is not possible to, as you say, "stop the clock." However, it is quite possible to fix that clock so it works differently or design an entirely new system of keeping time.

L: So it's not up to God to help us with infertility? It's up to scientists?

G: For this is not what at all we are saying. What it is we are meaning to say is for all human problems of a medical nature, there is a solution. Collectively, as a whole, your healers of medicine can and do desire results based -anthropy, meaning they seek to find a solution that serves the root problem of all illnesses all at once.

L: Well, wouldn't that root problem of all illness be one thing, the mind?

G: Well, yes. This is, of course, your answer. All illness is of the mind, and many of your doctors, healers, and scientists are beginning to see this effect of body-mind connection.

L: Some are yes, but certainly not enough.

G: Your skepticism is warranted now, but this is not to say some scientists cannot figure out what man hates he also creates within his temple.

L: Meaning the body.

G: Body is the only temple that one need dote on.

L: What are we doing wrong to our bodies? What systems were set in place that we are not following here?

G: We shall address this question in two parts. One must first understand how the body is designed and that it is to service an individual's conscious mind. For every portion of an individual's body functions from a standpoint of conscientious creation. One's view of oneself can and does affect how bodily functions either thrive and survive or breakdown. There is no in-between.

L: So when our bodies are showing signs of illness or fatigue, it is connected to how we are viewing ourselves or others?

G: Yourselves, yes. "Or others" we would say no from a standpoint that how one views oneself will be always in relation to the concept (for which we have not covered here yet) that all thoughts of another sister or brother are of harm only to oneself. How we view another relates to the way we are viewing ourselves. We say another is "fat," for that is the way we view our own bodies. We carry a victim-like tantrum of racial epithet throughout lifetimes calling ourselves ugly or unlikeable because of color of skin or class of citizen.

L: So we not only create illness because of what happens in this lifetime, but also because of these other simultaneous lifetimes' behaviors?

G: We have said that you are of all things at all times. Profiling and provocation of attacks on other beings like you strictly come from one's perception of one's failures in all lifetimes simultaneously. Therefore, it would be advisable to ask oneself, "Who am I?" in relation to other beings. "I am your brother" is the only correct response to such a question. For it is when we see brothers and sisters as one mind and perhaps one body (from a metaphysical standpoint) that we would see all illnesses disappear into the nothingness from which all of them came upon you all of your human race.

L: OK. But can we talk then about our current lifetime we are living in? Because while I get what you are saying here (and the reference to simultaneous lives), it's a whole lot of pressure to have on our shoulders to not create an illness in our body based on someone beating you up or being mean to you in

another lifetime (something that your mind, in the here and now, has zero recollection about). Know what I mean?

G: Yes, and we will now answer the second part of your earlier question about your health crisis, which your earth is now experiencing at levels of unfathomable rates.

L: I forgot my question. I had to go look back at it again.

G: And what was it?

L: In terms of our bodies, what systems that have been set up to keep us illness free are we not following here?

G: All systems are predicated first on one's own thoughts as we have just said, but this has many layers of which we will now speak. No body can or should have to withstand the high levels of consumption of the by-products of alcohol, drugs, cigarettes, or cigars. These are not of God or of Spirit the like. They are to be used sparingly by all who would partake.

L: What about pharmaceutical drugs that are meant to help and heal?

G: Pharmaceutical armistice has made it so one's body can withstand these elemental invaders.

L: Meaning?

G: Profitability aside for now, at the heart of medical science is a need for cures and an assurance that all invaders of unknown origin upon the body are deconstructed and assailed. This is to say our experts in science are, at the core, creating a structure of healing from a space of pure, unadulterated love for all mankind.

L: The scientists, perhaps yes; the corporations that are backing them, not so much. They are putting profit above all and frankly withholding cures, I believe.

G: As we speak further, a discussion of corporate profitability and responsibility will be debated later on. Let's continue with our discussion of one's body temple.

L: So what else are we doing wrong to the body system we have all created?

G: It is not so much what you are doing, but what you are not doing here that is at issue.

L: Then what are we not doing to our bodies?

G: Supplying them with the essential vitamins and minerals needed to sustain bone structure and flexibility and all manners of movement and ease upon joints and suspension systems.

L: And why is this lacking?

G: The food supplementation provided has been bastardized as a means to create profit for the very few who have no need for the supplementation that your poor, needy, and hungry require. Therefore, your food quality is substandard in providing what it is your bodies need to thrive and survive.

L: Which is?

G: Essential amino acids, niacin, thiamine, vitamins A, B, C, D, E, K, and B-12, plant protein, fruits, vegetables, water, sulfur and some salt.

L: Is that it?

G: The requirements are necessary to maintain harmony within the body systems, yes.

L: So we can't think ourselves healthy, then, if we are not eating essentially? Doesn't that negate the mind-body connection? Can our thoughts affect our body if we eat poorly but think positively?

G: A good question indeed. We are such big thinkers of body consciousness, yet we know nothing of proclamations of fundamental scientific principles, which create connections of cohesiveness between bodily functions. Minds alone may state a case for healthful functionality, but scientific principles are always at play here.

L: Huh? I don't understand half of the words here at all. I think I need to go to medical school first.

G: There is no need, for all already know all of what we know. The remembering is what is hard for you. We shall explain another way.

All functionality of one's body dynamics requires certain elements, which one must provide in order to keep one's provided body churning at full functionality. A breakdown occurs on a psychological or mind level when one's thoughts are not of God, Spirit, or a conscious space of Love's presence. This does not mean one may bypass said elements, which are, as repeated above, water, sulfur, amino acids, niacin, thiamine, and vitamins A, B, C, D, E, K and B-12 as well as a few other nonessential but primary elements on which bodies thrive.

L: Such as?

G: Calcium carbonate, alkali, unrefined and unprocessed cane sugar, plant protein (particularly from ground sources).

L: Well, now science believes sugar to be terrible for you and as addictive as some hard-core drugs.

G: This is not true, nor does it bear repeating, as above. All unprocessed means of the obtaining of sugar are acceptable.

L: But don't we as a planet consume too much sugar in general?

G: It is simply a matter of taste and not substance. A substantial amount renders one unable to fight fatigue and fat but does not harm one's core body system.

L: And what of the processed kind of sugar?

G: One need only understand how chemical compounds of a foreign nature scientifically affect one's biology to figure out why these processes are of a nature that is harmful to body functionality.

L: Just to be clear and explain it in more simple terms since you completely confused me earlier. Yes, our minds do create illnesses by our conscious and unconscious thoughts and actions. However, on a scientific or medical level, we still need to be feeding ourselves the essential elements regardless?

G: You have hit the nail on the head.

L: And if we don't feed ourselves the essential elements, then what?

G: Then your bodily functions, while they will not necessarily create specific diseases in one's experience, are of a lower energy vibration and thus unable to provide the necessary and quality brain function one needs for optimal mind-body creation.

L: And without optimal mind-body function is how we manifest diseases?

G: This is extremely accurate, yes.

L: So this also speaks to the junky processed food and beverages we consume in mass quantities and the chemicals we not only grow our food with but cake all over our produce after it's been picked. What should be done about this chemical warfare we are waging on our bodies?

G: For one only need understand how bodies function for avoidance of subordinate invaders as such intrusion would supply.

L: Intrusion?

G: Intrusion of substantive creations of compounded chemicals will thus then create disorder within one's own temple.

L: How can this be avoided when companies are irresponsibly putting our lives at risk?

G: We are not here to blame nor judge, for we observe only. There is, however, no good reason for the production of chemical compounds for creative realization of mass quantities of food supply.

L: So we should not be dumping chemicals into and all over our food and produce?

G: Certainly not. From a spiritual perspective, there is no good reason at all for bastardizing one's supply of food by way of chemical concentrations of acids and antibiotics and nitrates and casein and carcinogenic matter, which via mass consciousness, lead to a molecular cancer causation on a global scale.

L: Thank you for that. I wish more people would understand this mind-body connection when it comes to our food right now. One of the most frustrating relationships I have is with a young woman who is so delusional in her thinking (because of her past) that she has created perceived illnesses for herself and alienated most around her. I do not know how to break through to her and help her. What may I do to help her?

G: You need do nothing my dear. It is not upon you to heal anyone. This you do not yet understand. Use our words as a means to bring salvation only to yourself, never to another. For only one's self is capable of a radical shift in his or her own perspective. Nonetheless, one shall take anyone under one's wing sent to them, as long as listening is as much a part of the equation, as it necessitates God's heeding or lack of ignoring anyone's call for help. For only then are we able to answer the call together.

L: So when someone comes to me for help, I need to listen to the problems but call upon God and Spirit's help?

G: Before speaking back, always.

L: This is many times easier said than done. People, the humans of earth, get so caught up in their drama. And let's be honest, these illusionary-based worlds we create for ourselves can really suck the life out of you. I can see why those who are in poverty and pain can get stuck in their mindsets. I have not a clue how to help them.

G: It is not up to you, for helping everyone is not your function upon our earth. It is upon all beings and creators to heal themselves.

L: But I want to help people. I want to wake people up and allow others to have a happy life too.

G: And are you currently living a happy life, as you say?

L: Not exactly, no. Not yet anyway but I'm trying.

G: And you will get there but why, then, would one focus energy on the healing of others prior to healing oneself?

L: I guess that's true.

G: A goal of salvation for oneself shall be one's only mechanism for true healing of all other brothers.

L: Heal thyself, and then heal the world?

G: No. Heal thyself, heal thy world within, and then, and only then, may the outer healer shine through.

L: Well, when will I know that I have healed myself and my inner world?

G: You will know when one has spoken my words consistently by priding oneself on knowing God and knowing oneself to be in the image of God, by speaking and acting consistent in its present moment reality.

L: So consistently acting and speaking in a matter that serves—

G: Your higher purpose, which is to know God. Spirit can, will, and does remind you each and every day of this purpose. It is, however, upon one to heed these magic moments as much as one possibly can.

L: It felt earlier that our conversations were easier and flowed more quickly to me. I feel as if getting the words out is more difficult now. Can you explain why this is so?

G: For to hear us is to know one's own truth. We need remind you of only that which you already know inside of you. One's own fear, however, may stretch the present moment story of one's life further than it need be.

L: So when I am holding onto fear—

G: Or anger or resentment—

L: I have a harder time hearing my own truth and am prolonging the information that we all already know from coming through?

G: Precisely.

L: So then it begs the question as I attempt one day to publish this material, whom am I talking to exactly here? God, Spirit, angels, myself, or someone else, such as Dr. Peebles?

G: We shall address Dr. Peebles later. First, we will say again and again you are not not speaking to God. You are, however, a conduit (as all are capable of being and doing and having a conversation such as this) of spiritual principles carried through your own voice as if you were God in your own self-image.

L: After all this time, then, I am not speaking to God? I am speaking to myself?

G: As if you were God. For God is within all of us. Therefore, when you are writing my words, my truths are your truths, are all of our truths. As we have said many, many times in many, many ways and places, we are one, all of us.

L: Is the human race truly hundreds of thousands of years old?

G: According to the laws of time and space as dictated by the calendar kept upon earth. For in heaven, one's timekeeper is much more accurate.

L: Well, that explains why we have been able to live more lives than our calendar would allow.

G: Lifetimes (albeit sequential and simultaneous) heretofore are not accurately represented by calendar nor space-time.

L: Meaning what?

G: You are of this world but also of another world, as much as all of your beings on earth are the same makeup.

L: When do I go back and erase all of this?

G: Now why would you want to do that?

L: Because it seems all very preposterous and frankly ludicrous at times.

G: When fear enters our mind or worries, doubts, and other nonsensical and irate emotions, we may turn to our Father and God of heaven, the voice of Spirit within, and for that one instant, all irrational, nonsensical notions will be erased by one simple prayer or asking. "Let us now forsake all irrational, fear-minded emotions and thoughts. For we accept love into our hearts and minds, Amen."

L: Is it really that simple, though? I find that even when I do turn inward and replace the thought with an instant prayer, eventually more unintentional bad thoughts arise later on, sometimes mere moments later on.

G: Human interactions dictate repeated scenarios. Moment by moment, inch by inch, whenever possible, return one's thoughts to Spirit. Whenever this repeated action is accomplished, a radical (if not entirely plausible to one's ego mind) shift occurs. One's system of energy replicates all prior processes of eliminating whereby a new, better pattern of emerging energy occurs within all of mind-body-soul creations.

L: Yesterday I was at the gym listening to *Conversations with God, Book Two*[13], and I literally jumped for joy when the Ten Commandments were mentioned. It was said there are no Ten Commandments. We spoke of this in the beginning stages of this book, and back then, I was really not at all sure if this was truly the case. When I heard that, though, I felt a sort of vindication, like an "I told you so" to anyone who doubted this.

G: Moses went up to the mountain. Of this you can be sure.

L: Nothing else?

G: What else is of historical and biblical significance. However, accuracy of a spiritual nature? No. We would not speak of this as a complete truth. Commandments are not of God, nor should they be spoken as righteous truth. For what is accurate is in the time of Egypt and its slaves, certain mandates were heeded as a means to follow a path out of a mindset of slavery, which your people believed in.

L: So what Moses heard was of God but meant for his people to follow as a way out of slavery, not as a way of life always?

G: Well, this is not to say certain notions are not necessary for one to follow as a means of knowing God. Truth and honor are doctrines of love consciousness. Love consciousness is one's only path necessary for release of slavery, be it now, or forty thousand years ago. The length of time does not matter here. Our referral here is to one's own mindset of enslavement, which has continued on for centuries upon centuries (in humanistic time-space) as all beings' minds envelope either with love consciousness or fear consciousness. For there is no difference between man's enslavement of another brother or one's own enslavement of oneself. The parting of the sea becomes possible when abject belief in one's own power to heal oneself through cocreation with Spirit is undertaken. By no other means may one deliver oneself from a slave state of being.

L: That's really good.

G: We know; we wrote it, together.

L: I fear I am still baffled by where all of this is coming from because I know very little of religion. Some of these words I have never even heard before, yet they are flowing out of me. So how can I be writing this when I know very few spiritual principles and even less, if anything, about religion? I have never even read the Bible one time. So any reference to that is totally above my conception.

G: Conception is a good word. One has no need for concept when one knows truth within. We are writing this book together.

All of us, as we think with one mind. It is only when separation of self occurs that cocreation becomes impossible.

L: So because I believe in the concept of one mind, that we are all God, so to speak, I am able to cocreate with all of us this information and material?

G: We are all of God. There is no thing not of God. "Of God we trust" is a more practical terminology than your current theology.

L: But I have heard that the only difference between us and God is that God created us and that we did not create God. So wouldn't that mean we are different?

G: God is a concept, not factual. Speaking of differences does not make truth either. A pillow is for the head, and this is a fact. A tree brings oxygen to your planet. Fact. All facts are easily and tangibly measurable. Measuring a mountain is possible. Measuring a being of all-encompassing, all-powerful, loving energy is impossible, in a sense. This is not to say we are not able to understand the need to document and measure what Source is. We are simply saying that we (God as you call us) are in all. And all means you and your son and your neighbor and the guy at the grocery store and your best friends and the man down the street and the lady who lives in Africa and the man who lives in Peru. We are in all at all times. There is nowhere we are not. It just is.

L: Throughout this book we have used the term God. Why, then, if this is not accurate would we use this term?

G: For many, God is a word that has distinct and purposeful

meaning. We do not dismiss the importance of God as a word to your sector of society that does use it. Remember there is no judgement in heaven. We use it as a means to connect on a basics level with all who choose to know us. Us being relative to We.

L: So then would you say to whoever sat down to write such musings as I have that connection is easier when it comes attached to the notion or concept of a godlike figure?

G: Figure, no. No one is up in the kingdom sitting on a magical unicorn throne dolling out million-dollar bills to good little boys and girls and bolts of lightning to bad ones. We are all just energy, renewable source energy. There is nowhere we are not. We cannot stress this enough.

L: And this source created us from itself?

G: Suffice it to say that when and once creation happened, there existed a moment when Source, from which all came, created itself unto another and another and so on and so forth as all God's (again, your word not mine) soldiers or creatures, children or minions, whatever word you so choose to describe it. That's the thing worth understanding here. No one word has the power of description unless a man or woman or child brings it to life. For such is the nature of all languages. It is worth notation that the word God comes from the Greek, ethos.

I paused wondering if this was true.

L: I had to look it up.

G: And what did you discover?

L: It applies here.

G: Of course it does. We will not steer you wrong here. Anyway, ethos meaning power of religious righteousness for all who seek it. Whoever is the most powerful shall conquer the weak, and what better than a God almighty to do such a thing? For hundreds and then thousands of people, God fearing belonged to the few who sought shelter from an unforgiving and cruel world. For fearing God meant having one to blame for life's injustices brought upon them. God fearing led to instantaneous corruption among leaders who burned and massacred any and all whose righteousness aligned nonsensically away from their own ideals. From their own summation of right thinking, wrong principles meant eternal damnation for all beings of light and love. Thus, then religion was born directly out of a fear mentality, which has stuck to this day within your society. Does that make sense?

L: I think so. In modern terms, basically the powerful leaders and those with the money used the term God to scare people so they would follow them blindly. When the people didn't, the leaders burned and/or massacred the people and blamed it on God punishing them and sending them to eternal damnation as a way to control their thinking and them? This sounds awfully familiar.

G: Not much has changed, has it?

L: Not at all. I mean we don't—Oh, wait. Yes. We do. There are still portions of our society that do this. It's quite sad really. We have barely evolved beyond our original ideals.

G: All who have come before you and all who will come after you have much to learn. Whenever a shift occurs in mass consciousness, a shift in world politics and presentation will occur.

L: But back to the word God. So the word just kind of stuck and has continued to resonate for thousands of years on earth?

G: Yes, and there is nothing wrong with this word as a concept. We have zero judgement on its interpretation. We seek only to inform and enlighten, on our behalf and at our behest, that all sound beings shall know universal truths from our ever-changing perspective, as all beings evolve. There is no one word to describe the indescribable. So one need only enjoy the miraculous abundant love from which he or she and all of us have come.

L: What then of something like *A Course in Miracles*[14], which uses the terms God, Father, Son, Holy Spirt, and of course, Jesus.

G: Yes, what then of it? As we have just explained, from a words perspective, the relatable nature of the context of said material is placed upon the one who is our writer. In a case such as *A Course in Miracles*, a terminology that reflected Christianity as a whole was underscored so as to appeal to a mass audience. Jesus and Holy Spirit were interchangeable as were God and Father and children and sons of God. Understandable language, as was inscribed by Helen Schucman (as was spoken to her through me), relayed a foundation for inner peace which, while perfectly acceptable when undertaken by said writer, has evolved further and beyond such limited thinking.

L: Is the course inaccurate, then?

G: Of course not. No pun intended.

L: Funny.

G: Many of our principles inside and around our book are perfectly accurate, as are many of the principles of the Bible and Quran. As we evolve, our understanding and complexities evolve. We, therefore, must inscribe from a new space, a new understanding. We have chosen for this one whose religious reasoning has no interference with our own words and reasoning. Whoever undertakes the reading of this material also may have no known affinity to a particular religious line of thinking or being. Although they may be born into a religious line of thinking perpetuated by their parents, they may have subconsciously or consciously begun to question its validity or sanctity.

L: So they probably won't be reading this in a church, temple or mosque one day?

G: It is quite doubtful. For your radical-minded thinkers (who are, of course, inordinately ordinary scribes) will undergo shame and ridicule from whoever seeks anything beyond enlightenment.

L: Especially when the Instagram, Facebook and social media trolls get ahold of this.

G: It will not matter. For one's own heart knows all truths. Beyond reason and madness is truth, and your own truth will set you free.

L: Amen to that. Who, then, is Jesus or the Holy Spirit in reference to in the course?

G: Spirit within. Internal teacher. Knower of knowledge. Seeker of truth and spiritual enlightenment. Master of wisdom and knowing. Jesus is you and me and we. He is all of us, and though you will not understand this, none of us.

L: Nope. Don't get that all.

G: You all will one day. On this you can trust us.

L: But Jesus was a prophet who "died for our sins," as religion has taught, and was nailed to the cross.

G: Jesus, a man who knew nothing of enslavement, sought only to share wisdom, compassion, empathy, and understanding. A being so enlightened, he was of no use to himself in your human world. Therefore, in his death did he enslave himself as teacher of all who came to him in asking and prayer.

L: Why would anyone enslave himself in the hereafter? Especially someone who never enslaved himself by negative thinking?

G: Jesus (thought only by way of name and foundational philosophy) as "slave" is the meaning of salvation. For in his salvation is his enslavement undone. One must return only to one's source of all knowing and being and undone from the cross will they be. As we cocreate, we are released.

L: So is Jesus then an OK term to use just like God. Kind of like whatever works for you, works for them?

G: Not necessarily. What works for some may not work for

others. Upon us you draw (as in name only); we will answer to all who knowingly return to our favor.

L: So essentially, we all come from the same energy or Source (which many call God). Jesus (as he was so named) is our spiritual teacher, or guide, who once walked among us but now dwells in heaven, and together we bring about salvation for one another? And individually we each have a soul?

G: Collectively each has a soul.

L: So not individually are we a soul?

G: We are all of a collective nature.

L: Why do we think as both individuals and collectively?

G: The design of the universe (and otherworldly planes) is such that each member or being has, at their disposable, the capability of acting and reacting to any and all circumstances whenever they are of body or other similar forms and functions. It is a means to remember who you are whenever you are separated from the source.

L: And we choose to do this as a way to grow and evolve the soul.

G: Precisely. So that I may know myself experientially, as we have previously inscribed in the *Conversations with God* books and material.

L: So you split yourself to know yourself.

G: Yes.

L: Why me? Why am I able to hear this and write this?

G: Why not you? Why not anyone of you? We have covered this ground before. Though from a perspective of mindfulness, there are some and only some who walk among your earth capable of such concentration and connection with Source.

L: And why is that. Was I chosen for this work?

G: Chosen, no. Inspired by and for would be more accurate terminology here. Chosen implies a specialness of which you are not. Not one of us is any more special than the other, of this you already know and comprehend. One's specialness and separateness cannot, will not, and should not be understood nor undertaken by those who seek universal truths. All who come to you are enlightenment seekers already seeking only to be reinformed and reintroduced to that of which already is known and understood.

L: Does it feel like we are going in circles a little bit?

G: Only when concepts are understood completely will we carry on further.

L: I think I am just confused by the whole Jesus thing. I get that God is just a word we use to describe where we all come from originally. God is the source of all of life, an indescribable

energy system. I just can't quite grasp the concept of Jesus and being enslaved as a teacher inside of us.

G: We will say it like this. All who know "God" know Jesus (his human name) too, as he is the speaker of truth, and injustices carried upon his back for all who "sinned" were remedied once his role was understood. For he could not live upon your earth longer than was needed to cocreate such an uprising that mass consciousness evolved to its current understanding of the God concept, which is to say all upon your earth then understood there is a presence and power from which we all emanated.

L: So Jesus's role upon earth was also to be a teacher? He was not meant to stay here permanently? Even as a human he was used as a learning device?

G: Even in human form he was a teacher of spiritual principle. Now, as a holy spirit, his essence lives inside all who seek to know God.

L: Are there other "holy" spirit guides?

G: There is only one Holy Spirit. There are, however, enlightened masters and other spirit beings who have ascended into our kingdom (which we call heaven) and walk among and above you as angels, guides, or spiritual teachers of truth. We are all encompassing all of the time.

L: "God" is a word we as humans coined, but what about heaven?

G: In the kingdom, there is heaven as well as many other places.

Relative to language skills, it is agreed upon for heaven as a concept to coexist here and on earth.

L: Great. Well, then I will still call you God here in this book because frankly it makes it a lot easier even though it's not a word I normally use.

G: What is preferable is practical.

L: My mind is spinning.

G: One cannot explain or comprehend in one evening what it has taken some a lifetime to understand. Your accomplishments on this front to decipher our often-difficult and unusual explanations are impressive.

8

God—The Interview, Part Three

"*Dear Universe, the Oneness, together we shall cocreate this book's material so that we may help awaken the masses and allow a shift in consciousness for all who come to experience these words. Amen.*"

Laura: This morning we woke up to the news that Donald Trump is now banning transgender people from serving in the military. I am starting to understand more and more how he is our new Hitler, especially when looking at how he wants to kill our current health plan ensuring millions will die, possibly, who go uninsured. What can be done here? How can we fix a broken system and a broken-minded man who is single-handedly destroying our country and our way of life?

God: I stand before you as true leader of the free world and declare all political actions are born of wrong-minded (wrong being your term, not mine), fear-based inhabitants of Mother Earth. No said military-based action is justifiable in the laws of the universe, of which your current leader knows nothing. Therefore, ones in power undertaking a political coup will rightly destroy your leader's policy indictments upon transgendered citizens.

L: So we should release all fear on this matter?

G: On this matter, which is of particular importance, yes.

L: If we were to undergo a shift in consciousness, a change in perception as a whole, what would one say in prayer here to help heal this national wound we carry in the form of Trump?

G: "Dear mighty, holy Father of all, we the people stand aside to allow a conscious shift to be undertaken as a whole politically so that all who congregate together in this country of America be joined together as one mind—one perpetual partner in humanity—and draw upon its ideals to change perceptional policies, which serve others only as a means to serve themselves from a standpoint of power, money, and monopolizing madness." For one need only remind oneself consistently of this prayer and practice to undertake radical-minded awareness.

L: How on earth could we get 275 million Americans to do such a (what some will see as absolutely crazy) thing as pray for a better world?

G: Why can't prayer be a daily practice? For some it already is. We simply must ask ourselves what is more important, peace within or peace without?

L: Why can't we have both? Why can we not have peace within and peace in our world?

G: You can, very much so. However, it is upon each individual conscientious being or person to unseparate, that is to say not see himself or herself as a separate being but rather an equal to all. Whoever collectively undertakes said notion thus will then radicalize more beings of a submissive nature, and that domino effect can and will change world views.

L: One person can change the world who submits through daily prayer such as above?

G: One person cannot no, only one mind. There are, however, those who are among the citizens of Earth whose radicalized notions and perceptions have broken through to sectors of society ready for mass change and a global phenomenon. Deepak Chopra, Oprah Winfrey, Wayne Dyer (when he was alive on earth), Gabrielle Bernstein, Neale Donald Walsch. Mahatma Gandhi and Mother Teresa, when they were inhabitants. These are some within society. It is upon all beings of light, raisers of awareness, to shift perspective out of one's mentality of fear-based life to a mentality of love-based life. Once a shift of consciousness is undertaken, one by one, attitudinal democracy begins to take hold, which creates an unseen affect within other beings.

L: So if one person prays for a massive shift in consciousness, other minds will come to join it, even though they have no idea this is even happening?

G: One cannot underestimate one's own personal power system within.

L: Let's move from serious topics onto more relatable topics of everyday life here. We are a society obsessed with self-image,

and so we poke and prod at ourselves and get plastic surgery to fix what we don't like. Why can't we accept ourselves for who we are, and is it wrong to change our faces and bodies the way we do?

G: It is not wrong mindedness from which all suffer foolish behaviors of self-defacement. Rather, it is perception of wrongful anecdotal incompetence from which all who come before you are born.

L: I have not one clue what that means.

G: What it means is for anyone to see oneself as holy and just in body form, one would have to first know how body and mind relate to each other.

L: Which is how?

G: This is to say one's own body does not justify its need for world domination ("world" being internal world), nor does beholding one's own perception of mind-body concentration apply here.

L: I really don't understand what you are trying to say here. May you please speak in more simple terms here?

G: We will say it this way. When one's body first came into being, a potentiality was available (from the beginning of time as time became on each planet) to choose that which appealed to one's sensibilities. As humans evolved, perception also evolved, whereas one's body, which used to be a thing of glory no matter what vision of it took place, is now in one's vision far less glamorous than those of his or her ancestors. We constantly seek to change our appearance as we move forward in the time-space continuum. Does this make more sense?

L: I think so, but I don't understand what wrongful anecdotal incompetence means.

G: We are glad you asked. It means simply that what you see is not what you get always. Attention grows where energy flows, and whatever you wish to see inside or outside is that which you will see. As bodies go, it was better to have no mirrors to look upon.

L: So once we invented mirrors, we began to see ourselves differently?

G: Precisely, my dear Watson. You do understand now?

L: Yes. Thank you for the clarification. Why can't you just say it like that in the first place?

G: For then you will never know that which is truth and that which is of ego.

L: Understandable, I guess. It's just hard to decipher sometimes what you mean with these oddball phrases like "anecdotal incompetence."

G: Then one must ask for clarification as you have asked before in other times of confusion.

L: All right, it was once mirrors were invented that our self-

esteem and self-image of the body took over. You did not answer my question though of if it's wrong to get plastic surgery to change your appearance if you don't like it.

G: We see nothing wrong in changing one's perceptive appearance, as wrong is a concept we cannot and will not ever comprehend.

L: There is no judgement on someone who wants to do this?

G: Judgement is only of other beings who are not of God currently.

L: So humans?

G: And other species, yes, who are not yet enlightened enough to know of judgement-free living.

L: But isn't all this—the plastic surgery and Botox and fillers—bad for our bodies and, frankly, for our minds and psyches? Shouldn't we all love ourselves for who we are on the inside and not the outside or body? Isn't this what mindfulness is all about?

G: One must comprehend how body and mind relate to one another for understanding of why fixing oneself externally becomes so important. "Of ego."

L: Of ego?

G: "Of ego" is how one views his or her bodily extensions. "Of ego" is one's driving force for "fixing," as you say, what is wrong whenever one looks upon a mirror. "Of ego" is the single most connective tissue, so to speak, that makes one's appearance feel as if it is not good enough. Therefore, one always seeks to change oneself whenever "of ego" strikes. For this is why billions upon your planet spend their money on such pursuits of hair, makeup, nails, groomers, plastic surgeons, weight loss products, dietary programs, and all forms of bodily transformation to fix themselves in service to ego pursuits.

L: What's wrong with wanting to be pretty or attractive?

G: As we have said before, many times, right from wrong is not of God; it is of ego. Therefore, it must be up to individual consciousness to decide what is wrong, from a standpoint of that about which we are speaking right now, which is body appearances.

L: It's up to us to decide if we see it as wrong or right as God holds no judgement on it either way?

G: Yes.

L: But shouldn't we get rid of the ego here and just be happy with our appearance as it is?

G: What question should be asked is, "How can we view ourselves differently?" not what is the thought about it.

L: How can we view ourselves differently?

G: Simply by asking God and Spirit within. Your hair is coming out, yet still you have not asked for help on this except for "volume" to be added. This is fine but does not address underlying thoughts and beliefs adding to the condition.

L: What should I be praying about?

G: "Dear great Father of heaven, upon earth I have undertaken the notion that my bodily appearance is of great significance to those around me. In asking for "volume" to be added, I have only masked the hidden beliefs of unworthiness. Allow me to see worthiness in abundance, and only then will I see worthy pursuits before me and allow voluminous locks to appear in my reality. Amen."

L: You wrote that for me. How could I have known what to say?

G: It is not necessary you know what to say. We will always say it for you in your asking. Intentions are a form of prayer, and yet they are not exactly the same. They are merely goals to be accomplished from an ego's perspective. This is not to say they do not have value. However, whoever undertakes intention coupled with prayer truly has the keys to the kingdom, so to speak. Therefore, once prayer is undertaken in commune with God and Spirit, we are knowing already what it is that all want. So there is no need for your words. Ours will suffice. Remember there are ladders of prayer, and until all reach a level of prayer that seeks not to gain but to receive (that which is already available), only then can they truly have what they desire, not what they want, as those are very different needs. To desire is to have what is already yours. To want is to need, and need is a word that means seeking that which you think you lack. Lack is insufficient, and to be insufficient would bring upon more insufficiency. This is what we call your law of attraction. That which is like unto itself is drawn.

L: Back to a different topic. It feels as if whenever I do try to share my story, it doesn't really get very far or to the masses at all. Everything I do always seems shrouded in mediocrity. My whole life in fact has felt like a mediocre journey. I had a mediocre upbringing, very middle class. I had a mediocre career—better than some but worse than others. I had a mediocre love life—again better than some but worse than others. Just kind of "stuck in the middle."

G: This is a lot of questions to throw to us at once. Let us first take the notion of sharing you have mentioned here. A story of which you had written (with a point which you hoped to make) is necessary, though this does not mean all who come to it will accept it as truth. Much of what you are writing will go largely unnoticed, as it goes against what many still at their core believe to be true. Within all of us, of you, is a good, honest, decent human. The "without" part is where humans get Trumped (as this is related to a post you shared on your president). What's happening in your country is a reflection of direct-minded ideals, which have and will always be in place until and unless there is a group-minded swap of ideals. The ideals that initially came to pass no longer apply in this current evolution of society. "We the people" does stand for nothing more than "we the government" currently. There is no right-minded thinker among current leaders, which has led astray all who seek to bring about and draft laws in keeping with the evolutionary nature of change among your people. Most are still stuck in the dark ages of "be seen and not heard" for fear of being gobbled up by lions or tigers, trampled by elephants, or worse. There can be no movement out of a deep-rooted fear unless one seeks to exchange one's thought processes for those of one's one and only source of lightness and being.

L: So part of what holds us back from evolving as human beings is our initial fight or flight response from way back in, like, the caveman era?

G: Has not much changed in your world? Well, yes, you may have lights and airplane transportation, cars, and scooting mobiles which fly a little bit, but what you don't have at all is peace among a civilization that was born from peace and from love. One only needs to look to a caveman to understand there is not one difference in our fear modalities, which evolved only out of an irrational notion one could be harmed by such creatures as had been placed among you. Do you believe an animal can attack? Why, then it will. Do you fear an army of one, such as your president, may attack? Why, then it will. Injustice is injustice whether brought upon by one's own fearful thoughts or not. The time stamp does not matter, for it is all one's own manifestations, which he or she has brought upon and to oneself, just as in the era of the caveman. All who come to know love will have no need ever of hate. Whenever you share something, remind yourself that in the sharing of it, you must only seek to know yourself, and then, and only then, shall it be truly seen by others. Whether they agree or disagree shall be none of your concern. Only the information being shared is of importance. We can discuss your fear of mediocrity now, and forever we shall move away from a topic that does not serve you and that is the pursuits of the ego.

L: Before we go there, can I just mention that my post about our president, which certainly and very earnestly came from love, had been liked by only seven people and shared not one time. Yet post a selfie or photo of my son and seventy or eighty people like it. This is what is wrong with our entire society right now. Self-imagery and self-promotion is lauded, while soul awareness is largely and subsequently ignored by

most, if not all. This makes me sad and also begs the question why even write a book if only a few read it and even fewer understand its core message?

G: Why not do anything, then? Why fear having or being what you say you have wanted here in this lifetime?

L: Why would I fear that?

G: Why wouldn't you want to be or have those things on which you have placed great importance? Why bother, then, to ask?

L: I want to be those things; I don't fear them. At least, I don't think I do. Do I?

G: Our greatest fear is not what we are but what it is we can become. For when we have all that we desire, then perhaps there will be nothing else. A lonely island it will be when all who have gathered upon it are in an awakened state of being. For one who seeks enlightenment may be only one of a few who appear on God's green earth.

L: Well, yes. It is frustrating being "not special, but different" and seeing the bigger picture when so many others do not. I'm not sure it's fear, but it is certainly anger and frustration of being unable to break through to more people.

G: You cannot awaken those who do not wish to be awoken.

L: Well, my fear is that I have poured my heart and soul into writing (sorry, cowriting) this book, which I very much wish to share and have it be read and understood so others will

"join me on the island," I guess I would say. I want to live in a peaceful society where no one is downtrodden and beholden to anyone else.

G: You will. One day. But here and now it is not possible; therefore, one must remind oneself every day, persistently and consistently, of his or her true nature. This and only this will grant inner peace. True wisdom need not be shared to be understood by the many; it need only be understood by the one who undertakes such a prospect.

L: That doesn't address the underlying notion that once I submit this material it will largely just be ignored.

G: And if it is, then so be it. Who am I? Who are you to judge the actions of others? As we see fit to enhance our own manifestations of joy, love, or abundance, so we shall reap the benefits for ourselves. It matters not who reads this, only that as you write it you benefit. It is a goldmine for all who seek the riches, rewards, and inner sanctity of truth and justice. Is that not the American way? We fear what we do not understand. For some will and do find all of this blasphemous and shameful. "How dare certain liberties be taken in sharing God's Word. For this is a God you do not understand. You have never been to church or temple," they will say. And yet you, who are spirit awakened and enlightened, are no longer threatened by notions such as disdain, self-righteousness, bitterness, anger, resentment, and any and all attacks on love (which you all are and always will be and have been). No wonder there is fear, and for this we do not judge; we only understand. For there is no need to fear, for fear shall hold you back from publishing something so vastly important. One needs only to find an audience of one who is willing to listen. One who is willing to listen breeds another who is willing to listen and so on and so forth. Until our words are heeded and understood, no one can and no one will benefit more than you will from it. When a point has been reached whereby attacks yield nothing upon the soul, then you will share this willingly and openly with whoever is wanting of it.

L: But if no one but me ever reads this, then I alone will have benefited.

G: You will share it, for we know within you, within your soul, is the heart of a spirit warrior born again to condemn herself and finally (after many lifetimes) relive condemnation and then revert from its clutches a new, more evolved, triumphant being of light. Love replaces darkness, and for all of time, you will now walk in glory to your maker and rejoice saying, "I have risen from the ashes. I alone cannot change the world. I alone cannot change my world. I alone do nothing alone, for I am of God, and God is of me, and together may we create a peaceful inner world whereby a peaceful outer world may be possible for all, if not for my brothers and sisters and all who are children of Source Energy. Amen."

L: Back to my question of mediocrity. Can we address this please now?

G: Well, let's say hello again, then, to your ego, which rears an ugly head now and again in you.

L: I get that my ego sees me as having lived a mediocre life, but I can't escape the fact that my love life, my career, and my home and financial situation have always been medium size,

kind of like a McDonald's french fry. The small is good. The medium is OK, but most people want a super-size life.

G: Let's look upon your life now. You have had many, many great loves. Is this not so?

L: That is true. I have, but none that stuck around too long.

G: We addressed this earlier; shall we go back?

L: No. It's not necessary. I get it.

G: You have had many wild, exceptional experiences, such as your time on *Access Hollywood.* Oscars, Emmys, parties, Super Bowls, and others are projects you deemed dream-like opportunities.

L: True.

G: Have not others been unable to ever partake in said activities?

L: No. There are not a lot of people.

G: Your home, which we have chosen for you, is it not beautiful and large, filled with light (as you had requested) and perfectly capable of housing your son and yourself in luxuries few others enjoy such as a swimming pool or a community of like-minded beings who gather together frequently for parties and play time?

L: True, again. And I very much get what you are trying to say here, but none of this has come as—

G: You are going to say easy.

L: Yes, easy. None of this has been easy. I have had to work hard my entire life to have these things. I have struggled, and I have worked my butt off and yet still find myself in the same position over and over while others of "like-mindedness" get more and more. I'm not downplaying what I do have, just that it's not as if I am sitting around eating bonbons here and living off of my millions. I have to work just like everyone else to pay the bills and survive. I have been lucky, at least, to be smart enough to be able to work, but if I am being perfectly honest here, I don't want to have to work this hard, and I am sure most people don't either unless they are doing something they absolutely love that brings them passion and fire and purpose.

G: And what are you doing now?

L: Something that brings me passion and fire and purpose?

G: Well, amen to that. You see, my dear, most upon your planet are not doing what it is that brings them joy or happiness. They are doing what it is that brings them financial gain. Only does one truly gain when worldly purposes or possessions are cast aside. For one's purpose is one's power. We all have a purpose, which is that we grow and evolve. However, whoever seeks to only achieve wealth and status misses purposefully creating from a space of true knowledge and wisdom. When we speak of career, when we speak of work, we choose typically words of enslavement or misery. Whoever is speaking of commitment to anything should always relay thoughts, words, and feelings that are of a higher vibration. "I enjoy what I do." "I get to work." "I bravely choose to honor my commitment to a company that serves a purpose different from my own."

L: This is all well and good but doesn't resonate for the entire world of humans who need jobs to pay their bills and keep a roof over their heads. Most are struggling to survive in this world, and many go hungry each and every day.

G: You are now heading back to—shall we say—you have hit the nail on the head here which is that mass consciousness dictates what one must achieve in this day and age to survive. Poverty is not of God. Poverty consciousness has guided your masses for centuries, since the idea of barter was invented by one's earliest ancestors. You were not born of lack, nor shall you or any of your world's inhabitants be forced to stay in lack and substantive impoverished notions. No beings who undertake specialness shall release unto others the ways and means of worthiness. For to share one's wealth would imply one's worthiness is no longer special or sanctified. Those of a wealthy nature seek impunity from the presence of God in their lives. Their beliefs of being "special" bind them to a God who they believe is doling out dollars for denigration and sanctifies only those who are of a worthy nature and "good stock."

L: So they think that God only gives a few bucks here and there to the meek and unworthy and riches to the most worthy men? Whenever I try to bring up my own problems, somehow you always bring it back to—

G: Worldly pursuits. Yes. This is by design. For all problems are worldly problems. Not one is more special than the other. Whoever deems a problem for himself damns it to all others. This is to say that as one thinks, so shall all be.

L: So if we complain of poverty, it spreads?

G: Like a virus, yes, throughout humanity.

L: Is this why things like autism and infertility seem to get worse?

G: Yes, exactly. For when someone decides for themselves a sickness has overtaken them, it then is shared by thought, which manifests itself upon an entire universe. Remember here all minds are joined as one. Therefore, no one of you thinks a thought to yourself. "To thine own self be true,"[15] is a misnomer. The real truth would be "To thine own self be thoughtful and kind so all others may be the same."

L: We really can't think any thoughts and not have it become a part of our world view?

G: All thoughts are active. All thoughts are powerful. All thoughts create form on some level, as we know you have read, and what that means is creation never stops. It whispers from another to another to another and can only be stopped by prayer, intention, and mindful escape from earthly endeavors.

L: But you just said creation cannot be stopped but then said it can be stopped by prayer and intention?

G: Stopped as in vibrational energy transformed into the nothing from which it came. A powerful idea can be broken down piece by piece, bit by bit until its worthless nature is revealed. Once revealed, the energy is replaced and a new system of energy takes its place. This is what you call manifestation. It is through prayer, belief, and intention that all manifestations arise. This is "God's" law. Without prayer, intentional goal setting, and practiced stillness, thoughts will bind one to his destiny.

L: We choose our destiny, though. So does that mean we can change our destiny?

G: Who told you that destiny is a choice made prior? This is not wholly accurate. Choosing one's destiny is like choosing a line at the candy counter. Shall I take the line for the chocolate bars or shall I take the line for the ice cream scoops? Either choice is good, and neither is wrong; it is, rather, one's own thought system, which allows for the decision. At any time however, one could choose neither and decide for nothing and walk away. We all have free will. Destiny is as much a choice as the candy aisle is. "I'll have what she's having."[16] (We like this cultural reference very much.) What she is having might be good; what someone else is having might be even better, but it is what I decide that is of most importance. A choice for love will always bring upon thoughts and feelings that serve one's highest good. A thought for fear has despair and damnation and eternal justifications for sinfulness. We see nothing wrong with your choices (and by this we mean all of you). We are simply saying choices have consequences for all in the illusional world in which you all are living. From this point, we shall make yet again the point that fear is a choice to view that which is false. To change this, we must renounce falsities in exchange for truth, and to do this, we must undertake radical measures for prayer and intention on the daily.

L: What about the "holy instant."[17] Can we really transform a thought instantaneously by giving it back to God or the Holy Spirit?

G: Immediately. Yes. You may desire a new result, but this happens only with a sturdy application of focused prayer and intention coupled with a belief in one's own power of cocreation. Alone we can move molehills, but together may we move mountains.

L: How do we go about finding our true purpose, especially when working to pay the bills often just gets in the way here?

G: One reminder here is for purposeful creation, to engage one's purpose is what must first be understood. To understand one's true purpose is to know oneself completely and fully. Take a Michael Jordan or Tom Brady, who knows instinctively what it took or takes to be a champion (or at the level of champion). He reminds himself each and every day of what makes him tick. What makes a goalie, a hat or dress maker, a candlestick maker, a princess party maker, a teacher, a doctor, a lawyer, or any other professional pursuers do what he or she does each day? Instinct. Pure gut instinct. A core-level gut reaction, which, when one doesn't do the thing that makes them tick, has them wondering why they are not doing it for passion or career goal.

L: Yes, but what about someone who dreams about being a rock star or a ballerina?

G: A true ballerina feels within her soul that she is meant for dancing. A true musician partakes in music to feed a longing, not to feed his family. A true artist practices painting for sheer exhilaration of creating a masterpiece or work of art. No one undertaking purposeful endeavors will ever feel the pursuit is not worthwhile. For in pursuit of one's purpose is where practical magic is attained. One need only return to God whenever partaking in passions for magical attainment of inner peace. Your purpose is your peace or, rather we shall say, where you are most at peace. Whenever and wherever you are at peace, that, my spiritual warrior, is your "purpose."

L: I feel at peace when I am writing but also when I am dancing or laughing, gathering with friends or sharing love, and being with my son, of course. Obviously, those things are what bring us joy, but that doesn't pay the bills. Do we all have a purpose that enables us to make a living here?

G: All beings have but one role to play, which is to say we are all here to grow and evolve. In remembering who we truly are, one's true purpose can be revealed. This is how you attain inner peace, which, as I have said, is your true purpose.

L: I have heard that we are each one of something, like healers or artists or tradesman. For instance, I have been told by many psychics that I am a healer. So there is a part of me, and I guess I would call it a gut instinct, that believes this to be true.

G: Then it is true for you; you become what you believe.

L: But why, then, does someone become a doctor, a lawyer, a baseball player, an artist, an actress, a builder, etc.? Many people will say they felt "a calling" to do something, which leads me back to the question of purpose as well as the earlier statement you made about following your gut instinct. Instinct is why a champion becomes a champion, and all of that we have covered.

G: We have covered a lot of ground here. One notion (which has not and will not change) is that the attainment of inner peace is your purpose here on earth as well as in heaven as is also to know yourself as I know myself, as we are all of one mind. This is spiritual truth and universal principle. Uncovering what makes you tick, why, this is simply "of ego." This is not to say which pursuit or career path you take isn't meaningful or important for you. However, instinct is a guidance system we have given to you all for purpose of separating fact and fiction. The fact is you each are capable of being a Michael Jordan, an A-Rod, a Tom Brady, a Misty Copeland, a J-Lo, your swimmer Michael Phelps, or your gymnast Nadia Comaneci. Instinct merely predicates or "pre" dictates where practice shall be applied in the achievement for such a goal as to win a Super Bowl, climb Mount Everest, pop a fly ball, or perform in *Swan Lake* in front of an audience of spectators. Performance pre-dictates perfection. "Par for the course" reminds us never to attempt to defeat an opponent without first listening to instinct or else defeat is rightly imminent. Of this all of your greatest competitors know. Instinct indicates which lane to take, which way to turn, which drive to make, which song to sing, or which note to write. It is a route map for all to download whenever one feels guided to do so.

L: So is instinct of God or of ego?

G: For this is a great question. Instinct is of ego and of God, for they work in tandem side by side. Of this you can be sure.

L: But I thought God and ego were at war and that we must rid ourselves of ego's attempts to poison us?

G: A question worth undertaking here for sure. Instinct of God is quiet and factual and never harms one's psyche or soul. Manifestations instantaneously arise out of instinct. "Shall I go left, or right? North or south? Back or forth? The phone rang, shall I answer it? Where shall I hide the presents? What time should I leave for the party, and when should I come home?"

L: I get that. Everyday, mundane types of questions arise, and our instinct is—

G: The GPS, which guides you there. Instinct of the ego moves one forward in the succession of life goals. "I want that car. No. I want that car. Oh, I like that one even better but which color to choose? I think I will go with gray because that's what my instinct dictates for me. I want to be a dancer or play football. Mountains are for climbing not just seeing. Wow, this song is perfect to sing. This acting thing, I should give it a try. Hey, wait; I am really good at this. I should do more of it and audition for some roles. I love to cook, perhaps I am a chef?" Goal attainment.

L: I think I'm getting it.

G: "This right here, right now is what I want to be and do. My instinct tells me so. Oh, but wait a minute; I may not be good enough to sing, dance, or act. So instead, I will build houses, work in the mines, drum up business in sales, or partake in pursuits I dislike but that pay my bills." Do you see where I am going with this?

L: We put aside our earthly pursuits to purposefully pay our bills instead of purposefully pursuing what makes our soul and ego happy? But aren't we supposed to cast our ego aside in spirituality?

G: Ego pursuits of an earthly kind are never black and white.

Perhaps we may speak of this later on. For now, let's move on to more generic topics, such as painting one's nails.

L: Is that a joke?

G: Perhaps, yes; or perhaps instinctively you felt something was amiss and decided for yourself to question that which seemed odd and strange to you?

L: Perhaps, yes.

G: Ego mind instinctively stepped in saying, "Why on earth would we talk about painting our nails here?" Soul knows it is acceptable to talk about whatever we want with no judgement whatsoever about itself or anyone else. Ego is cautious and trepidatious and at times raucous and gung ho. For winning is an ego's true joy. Competition is instinctually based. Kill or be killed. Win, lose, or draw is the ego's name of the game. Dragon beats bear, just as panther beats parrot, or at least this is what you learned growing up. Instinctively, ego knows which is the weakest opponent and where to strike to avoid losing the battle. None of this is wrong or right, but rather, it is fact. The meek shall inherit the earth? "No way," says the ego. The meek shall be struck down and beaten to a pulp. "Winner takes all, and I am the true winner," says the ego. No one who instinctively drives the yards or bares the bullet can ever lose an ego's true mission to win at all costs. And that is why your Michael Jordan and Tom Brady and Tiger Woods and Ty Murray were at one point at the top of their respective sports games. It was pure gut instinct driven by ego pursuits. We will say again this is neither wrong nor right. "It is what it is," as you earthly wordsmiths would say.

L: Is that sarcasm?

G: Why, yes. We enjoy it now and again too, you know.

L: It took a long time to get to the point, but I do get the reference now. So thank you.

G: You are more than welcome. We are grateful for the time spent together in cocreation. For not many would undertake such a purposeful creation as what we are writing here. There is much more to uncover, for you this is only the tip of the iceberg, so to speak here. Your questions are many.

L: There is one big issue that arose today in me. I had a slight panic attack going back to Helen Schucman, who wrote *A Course in Miracles* and died of pancreatic cancer. After she died, people started attacking the book because it made no sense that someone who knew and wrote about what God's will was for us (and how to achieve it) would die a painful death from cancer.

G: First of all, we may say the undertaking we embarked upon with her took such a long time, and for her it was something she had never even heard of before. So her core beliefs were stretched beyond her limitations. Second, we shall say practice breeds purposeful creation. One who undergoes a transformation does not always stay in transformation. As soon as one goes back to ways of irrational mind, one suffers again. Miss Schucman, as we shall call her respectfully, surely had neither the will nor the wily spirit to continue her pursuits. While undergoing treatment, she needed only to have practiced what it was we preached through and to her to remove all blocks to abundant heath and prosperity.

L: So then the same goes for me here?

G: Of course. You cannot and will not escape the wrath of the downtrodden and weary. They will come at you with a force so mighty that it will feel as if ten men have jumped upon your chest and beaten you silly. It is upon you in that moment and that moment only to ask, "Dear God, our words, our meaningful phrasing has purpose, and in that purpose I proudly am able to share this with as many who will listen. For those unwilling to listen, allow any and all attacks I bear to be witnessed but never be internalized or demeaned by them. I walk in the light of knowing I am safe and guided by Spirit. Amen."

L: Well, OK, but if I am being honest, I have been feeling very strange lately, as if something has inhabited my body and is almost, like, physically dragging me down at moments making it hard to walk or even type. As if someone or something is taking over my body. Then I had this thought—

G: Irrational thought.

L: OK, sure irrational thought, that I would go out and share this book, and people would read it, and then a year or so after it's published, I would wind up with a brain tumor, and scientists will dismiss all of this as the musings of a sick person who had a brain tumor, in much the same way they dismiss psychic phenomenon and near-death experiences as scientific brain junk.

G: Let us be clear first and foremost. You do not nor will you ever have a brain tumor, unless free will takes over and you create said circumstance. From where we sit or stand (however you want to think of us), your health is perfect, albeit in need of tuning up from a dietary standpoint and emotional components residually leftover from divorce and distress.

L: OK, but I am a big believer in signs and messages.

G: Of this we know and have established earlier.

L: And early in the morning a woman was talking to me about her neighbor who had a brain tumor, a teenager. And later on in the day, I saw a license plate that said YOO SYQ. You sick. Thus, I had a massive panic attic that Spirit was sending me a sign of being sick and needing to go to the doctor immediately.

G: Interpretation is also nine-tenths of the law. Here we must explain your obsession with license plates, while adorable and cute, is not an accurate representation of a point we are trying to make. It is when we try to interpret our signs and messages that many times "of ego" comes along for the ride.

L: Yes, but I have been told there are no coincidences?

G: We are not negating this but rather stating, as fact, one must first look at all the facts before deciding as judge and jury upon something that affects one's psyche.

L: So that license plate wasn't for me today?

G: We did not say that. We will finish simply by saying, "You Suck."

L: Now I am laughing!

G: Of course, we are joking, but the point being "you sick" could very well have been "you suck" or "you psyche." Which of those seems more likely to have been a message for you?

L: You Psyche?

G: And later on, were you not reminded to look up a passage on spirit animals (particularly centipedes and iguanas, which you had recently seen in and around your house), which then led you to a definition of said word "psyche" explaining it came from the Greek meaning "soul" or "butterfly," and have butterflies not always been a thing of wonderment for you?

L: Yes. What could I have done in that moment to ease the panic?

G: "Dear God, I don't understand your message for me, although I know it is for me. May you please rightly interpret it for me?"

L: And that's it?

G: That is it, yes.

In the middle of the night, during the course of my writing of this book, my son woke up with terrible stomach pain, and I had to rush him to the ER. While there, we sat together and prayed and accepted healing and a perfect outcome. It turned out to be a blockage in the bowels, which resolved itself on its own.

L: Well, last night, or rather, shall I say, this morning was quite an interesting undertaking. May we discuss this now?

G: Yes. We can. What happened was neither tragic nor accidental, no?

L: No. Thank goodness.

G: And why do you think this was the case?

L: Well, it wasn't tragic because my son was OK, and it wasn't accidental, if you are speaking in terms of a fluke. Or are you focused on coincidental or—

G: By design? We mean did you not resort to your tool box, throw everything you know into one big heap, and use it consistently. Prayer, meditation (well you did the best you could there, we know this is hard for you), and constant breathing for your son's pain management and stress. "Hypnosis of a soul" would be how one's breathing practice would be described here. What have you learned here from a shared experience with a child?

L: We are of one mind? I was able to pray for and with him for healing?

G: Powerful is it not, to know one's own thought processes are connected as such?

L: Yes, but why put my child through this? Was it a test for me? A learning moment? I don't think it would be fair to put a little kid through pain just to teach me a lesson!

G: You are angry, and for this we are sorry. We mean never to upset, harm, or dismay anyone with our modalities of unlearning. It is, however, a powerful lesson undertaken for all who may face a similar situation. Harm cannot come if one instantly returns to one's source with prayer and intention. Intentional direction of spiritual resources is all one needs to elicit powerful healing modalities.

L: OK, but tell that to someone whose child's appendix bursts, which could have been the case but fortunately was not.

G: You are missing the point, my dear, and we know you know what it is, but you would rather have us reveal it here. One who undertakes a panic-driven, fearful path is led to feel and see what it is they fear most. You have heard, "You don't die from the disease; you die from the diagnosis," and here it shall be said, "You die simply by belief in one's own power to be destroyed." No more. No less. "But what of a child with cancer?" one wishes to ask us.

L: Obviously, yes.

G: What of it? Have we not shown to you how minds are connected? Fear begets fear begets fear. Surrounding oneself in company is often a death sentence for all mankind whenever company brings the rain and the floods and fosters a very real sense of fear in your seemly real (but yet immensely unreal) earthly worlds.

L: So you are telling me that if a child dies, it's the parents' faults too? Their thoughts had something to do with it as well? Tell that to all the parents on the planet who love their

children deeply to the core, and you are casting a massive burden on them. Plus, it's natural to fear losing a child.

G: Natural? It is not natural to fear *anything.* It is natural to love, to walk among each and every one of your brethren and wish to take care of each other at a core level. Just as you love your child is how all should love one another.

L: I get it, but it doesn't answer the larger question of children getting sick.

G: We have spoken on this topic before, right here in this material. Unloving, unselfish, unacceptable, unpopular, and unbiased we will never be. Only love is truth. Selfish means to love oneself is fully divine. Accepting all of life's magic is our purpose. Popularity is a myth perpetuated by the masses to serve our ego's tricks. Bias is a weakness from which only man and man alone suffers. Our truth is your truth. There is no death, only life eternal, and no one can suffer a fate that has not been chosen by them, for them, or to them. All minds connected, all minds responsible.

L: But if you are God, then you would be responsible too. So why would God want to be responsible for children dying and parents losing their will to live afterward?

G: It is not my responsibility to think your thoughts, only mine. I cannot take from you what you are not willing to give back to me. "Of body." This is how we shall say to you that whenever one incarnates to a body, that person is responsible for all actions and reactions involving one's body. Sent to each and all is an internal teacher, a guide whom you may call "Jesus" or "Spirit Guide" or "Purveyor of Peace" or anything else that serves your need to define the indefinable. When you are "of body," you need only return your thought to your maker for rightful presentation of what is truth, and fiction will no longer be top of mind. In that instant one's illusions will cease to exist (if not for a moment) should one then return to a thought of fear again. The process must then begin again. Thought. Resist. Release. Unacceptable should be any underlying thought that serves ego mind, which seeks only to destroy you from the inside out.

L: Well, then why even implant an ego inside of us?

G: I did not do this to you all. Only in your ancestral roots will you find this answer. Adam and Eve spoke of the Garden of Eden and declared their righteous refusal to oblige our ways of light and/or love. "You reap what you sow" is a rule of God (which cannot be destroyed or broken), and it was breached. Thou shall not partake in the eating of the apple. We know you do not know this story very well, so we shall explain it to you and, hereafter, other stories as well. Eve, whom I created in the likeness of myself, from which all of us are substantively created, had but one purpose, which was love. Coveting anything held no meaning whatsoever at the time of supplementative creation.

L: What does that mean?

G: For only one world existed at that time, a world you all call heaven. Eve allowed for thoughts that had not been yet undertaken. As such, in her wanting to partake of the forbidden fruit, her wanting brought unto her precisely that which she was asking for. An apple bearing her name called out to her as if to say, "Eat me." Desires manifested instantaneously. Her wanting of anything brought about an entirely new plane of existence, which many would call "hell." Chained to her choices by a rule of the universe, "that which is like unto itself is drawn," Eve had no recourse but to finish that which she had started.

L: So hell is this illusion-based world we live in right now?

G: There is no hell. It is a mere concept of creationism, which not only does not exist but also never was nor ever will be.

L: Well, amen to that.

G: Our story finishes with (as all who think they know it will remember) Adam bearing witness to the partaking of the tree and of the forbidden fruit. From this point on, "all hell broke loose." (We like that phrase very much, you know.) Forgiveness became concept as did guilt and sin.

L: This is the origin of original sin, which I do know a little bit about from *A Course in Miracles*[18].

G: Original sin is an error of judgement, a thought for something other than kindness and lovingness. It is a thought for one's own selfish gain. It is our ego. Our ego is where we bare the fruit of our agitations and exasperations. Our ego concurs with that which is dark inside of us seeking to trap our progress as we maneuver ourselves out of fear and back to love.

L: So we started out speaking of why children get sick and wound up talking about Adam and Eve. So, just to conclude this, can you explain how it all relates?

G: We shall. All minds are joined in heaven. When you are "of body," any mind that accepts and allows for heaven, God, or

Spirit is conjoined again in an instant, but only for an instant until such time when the ego's thought begins again. When anyone "of body" undertakes a mindset of fear, any and all minds surrounding that person may then join in this chorus of chaos unless one has undertaken a radical shift of perceptive philosophy of mind-body-spirit and/or God philosophy.

L: So this is why whole sectors of society are impoverished? We have to not only watch the thoughts we think about ourselves but also watch the thoughts of those in our lives? Words and thoughts are binding and can get tangled together with those of our loved ones, our friends, coworkers, neighbors, and the like?

G: Yes, this is true. However, in the case of a child, which we touched upon earlier, no one mind can implant in another mind the notion of death upon that child. For if that child has chosen a circumstance from which to grow its soul earlier and prior to incarnating, it will cease to exist immediately. We rightly have told you all who seek to know themselves must know both light and darkness, yin via yang. Only once may this tragedy (as you all would have it called) exist, and while it is hard on all, it is a portion of evolution that cannot, will not, and has not changed.

L: Well, I understand the notion of it, but, yes, it is tragic, and for that I am truly sad. So that means that in most circumstances—

G: Most if not all. Remember we are speaking of a millimeter percentage here, a once-in-one's-lifetime experience.

L: OK. Most times, if not all, can we change our circumstances,

especially a child's, when we join minds together in prayer as well as keep our thoughts of ourselves (as well as others) godlike?

G: Intentionally have you asked for my help in healing your fearful thoughts about the staircase?

L: Yes.

My house has an unusually large winding staircase, and when I moved in, I would have panic attacks about kids in the house falling.

G: Has one ever spoken of a tragic circumstance toward your son or anyone else coming into your home?

L: Well, I mentioned it to a couple of friends in my neighborhood.

G: No child though?

L: No.

G: And have you not forgotten about said circumstance?

L: Pretty much, yes, I have.

G: Intentional deliberate prayer created a result. How may we describe this in another way?

L: You don't have to. I get it.

G: "Just keep praying, just keep praying."

L: Are you singing and making a reference to *Finding Nemo*[19] right now?

G: We sure are. Do you like it?

L: It made me laugh.

G: Laughter truly is the best medicine.

L: I thought prayer was the best medicine?

G: It as well. However, one who undertakes righteous immediate prayer has no need for medicine, only healing.

L: Can we move on to my current problem?

G: Illusion.

L: OK, the current illusion I have is my knees. Specifically, my left knee, which for some reason is bothering me ever since I turned it wrong running something out to my new car.

G: Is there guilt that surrounds a purchase of a new automobile?

L: There might be some. Yes.

G: Is there a sense of wondering whether or not this was an improper choice?

L: There might be. Yes.

G: Is there a plan to help with this unnerving illusionary issue?

L: Turn to God. And what shall I say?

G: "Dear God, may you reveal to me all of my bodily functions as they relate to my mindset. Where am I holding onto fear? Where am I lacking financially? What choices have been made that surround me, keeping me stuck in reactionary patterns of abuse? Amen." So now show us what you see. You may close your eyes if you like.

L: Lightning struck after I ran out to the car. When I opened the door, I turned my knee; I heard the lightning strike and saw it out of the corner of my eye. I ran back into the house and thought, "Oh crap! What did I just do to my knee?"

G: And what else?

L: I just heard, "There is no better place than being right where you are."

G: What does that mean to you in relation to your car?

L: I hated giving up my old car from California and now having to have a Florida license plate, which means I am now officially a resident. I rather liked my California plates because they represented who I was and still wish to be, the girl from Cali and Hollywood, and now I am just like everyone else, no longer special, just ordinary.

G: And what do knees represent as you have read recently?

L: Pride and ego. So I need to transform my thinking about where I currently live? "There is no better place than being right where you are." I get it. I know it, but I don't like it here as much as I did in California. It's too hot and humid and—

G: And what?

L: And, I mean it's not that bad. I have friends. I do have some fun here, but I have guilt and shame over taking my son away from his adopted-father figure, and for that I hold onto stress and anguish.

G: Manifesting themselves as eye problems, knee problems, skin problems (especially on and in the ears), weight problems, and hair problems. Have we missed anything here?

L: Nope, you pretty much nailed it.

G: Nailed to the cross are thee.

L: I am.

G: Condemning oneself.

L: I am.

G: Partaking and participating in moral turpitude of desired outcome for the changing of said circumstance.

L: I had to look up what moral turpitude even meant, but yes, I am guilty of all of those things including not asking my cocreator for help.

G: And how shall we change it?

L: A prayer for inner peace and commitment to daily practice?

G: Ding. Ding. Ding. Let us pray together now. "Dear God Almighty, Keeper of all that is holy within mind-body-spirit, allow me to see the divine beauty within and replace misaligned thoughts of guilt, shame, and indignation. As we cocreate with one another, as we partake in shared mind, may we no longer pander to our egos. I am all that I am, for which I have no shame or regret. I act as God, for God, no more, no less. Amen."

L: Wow. That's good.

G: We know. We wrote it, together.

L: You say that a lot.

G: We do because its truth.

L: Earlier, we spoke of eating animals. I felt as if perhaps there was a contradiction, and I would like it clarified. You have said that animals have a soul as well?

G: That they do.

L: So then should we not be consuming them at all? It seemed as if earlier it was inferred that it is wrong to eat animals, but

later the reference was made to the fact that we are all getting sick because of the treatment of animals, not so much from the consumption of them. So which is it? Good or bad. Wrong or right?

G: We wish not to dwell here on this topic, for it is, as we have said, for an entirely other book. However, we will take the question, as it came and, therefore, must be answered. We see no wrong or right in consumption of animal by-products as such. One must understand, as we have said, animals have souls. Their souls are not unlike ours, however, they are no less than any other being. Yet they have been put on your planet for purposes of which there are many. It is, therefore, not required to consume or slaughter animals for sport, just as it is not required to be proper or improper. That which one chooses to make holy is what speaks to his or her needs. Animals are unholy to some and holy to others. "Thou shall not kill." One wonders why this has not applied to all living creatures as it has been to humans. Whoever sees a cow as holy has no need of consumption of said cow.

L: Holy cow. Is that where the phrase came from?

G: Exactly. Wherever one places importance and ethical value is how one's ideals about animals will shape their notion of them. We cannot speak of terms of wrong or right as application here, only as objective observers. Any animal originally living upon your earth was placed as a holy being as were you all. Survival of the fittest dictated a kill or be killed mentality, which continues to this day by humans. Animals of larger stature and smaller mind have become mass produced products unable to provide what it is humans actually need, which is proper nutrition.

L: Which we can get from plants and Mother Earth?

G: Precisely.

L: But because we do eat them is why we ended up speaking of them in terms of inhumane treatment and how that is now affecting anybody who does decide to consume them?

G: In so much as illustrated fact, yes.

L: So it is not of God to say whether the consumption of animals is right or wrong; it is merely to discuss the ramifications of doing it?

G: Fairly accurate, albeit difficult to digest for some.

L: Is that a pun?

G: Why, yes. It is.

L: It seems the further into this book or material we get, the more in depth the information is. Why is that?

G: We are wanting you first to understand easy concepts. Whenever this is accomplished, then one may further understand more difficult-to-swallow or grasp ideas.

I went away on vacation and then spent a week in lower energy dealing with work stress and not feeling able to communicate with the spiritual energy here. It was the day after the Charlottesville, Virginia, incident, where white nationalists rallied and protestors gathered against them. A young woman named Heather Heyer lost her life after a young man drove his car into the protestors.

G: You have much anger here.

L: How can you not?

G: We do not.

L: Yes. Yes. Yes. I know. No judgement. You only are observers of all the madness. Do you laugh at us ever for all the stupidity and chaos humans create?

G: Of course we do not laugh but rather seek to inform all of you at all times, always. It is not stupidity from which you all suffer; it is merely lack of faith in a system of energy from which all life forms begin.

L: Why can't we all tap back into that energy and create a better life?

G: Because you are not ready. Well, most of you are not ready. There are some, such as yourself, who are trying, have tried, and are winning. We feel you wanting to cry here, and we will say it is OK to express your feelings and emotions here for your current world circumstances. We will tell you this, however. No one who seeks to find enlightenment shall ever be lost. For we are with you at all times, in all circumstances, for all of time (and since the dawn of time). Your tears and your cries are heard.

L: But it feels most of the time our cries and tears are not being heard.

G: For this is not true at all, and you have learned this. We realize you are asking here not for yourself but for the readers of this material. So many of you have asked, and we have answered. Why send an army of one to share a powerful message during a time of crisis?

L: You mean the girl who was killed?

G: Precisely. Was she not a perfect messenger of peace?

L: All right, I am going to ask the question—

G: But you already know the answer.

L: Why did she have to die?

G: What message of hope ever has come from laying down the law rather than laying down one's own life?

L: But that was not her choice to die.

G: Wasn't it?

L: I don't know. You tell me.

G: Perhaps her role in the illusion was precisely what it was?

L: I get that from a spiritual perspective, but tell that to her family and friends. I guarantee only a small percentage of the billions on our planet would understand that concept. The rest of the world sees it as murder. She was murdered by a domestic terrorist.

G: In so much as he was a part of the illusion as well. He had a role to play as well. Each cocreated an experience from which the world (or at least Americans) can grow. This is what every experience, in everyone's lives, is all about, be it big or small, murder or madness, betrayal or betrothment. No one who ever seeks to understand the glory of oneself is incapable of creating such experiences of which you would call tragic. In actuality, they are not tragic at all but rather par for the course, as we have once said here before.

I spent the day contemplating our world and oddly enough watching Star Wars, *which I had never seen until recently. The message of the films is Love versus Fear, and yet I had no idea. Before I wrote, I prayed upon the creation of the book as I have many times.*

L: "Dear God and Creator, I am accepting that we cocreate this material together. May our words bind together to form a cohesive dialogue from which all can learn. Together we shall write, and together we shall remove words that are not of the highest good here. Amen."

G: Amen indeed. You are learning.

L: Why did I not know this about the *Star Wars* movie?

G: Never question one's timing in this lifetime.

L: The message is great, but what about the violent nature of the films?

G: Unnecessary but understandable considering nature's role in the universal structure of your world.

L: What does nature have to do with it?

G: Nature versus nurture is a studied structure within your society. It is natural to be curious about the world. We are nurtured at our mom's breast and through the words spoken and the love shown to us. It is the nature of humans to see violence as a natural expression. It is not natural to be violent. However, your current filmmaking standards believe this is the way to get the most bodies into the seats and eyeballs on the screen. So the nature of being attuned to violence has made it so all manners of movies, TV, video games, and other entities have it as part of their narrative. You would ask of us here, "Isn't it wrong?" And again we would say it is not wrong or right but rather what you make of it. If you view it for what it is, from a standpoint of love versus fear, well, then one can look upon it with a sense of wonder, "Aha. Well, that happened because that person was angry, enraged, empathetic, ill-advised and so on and so forth."

L: Are you able to watch our movies and TV shows and other media? Does God watch Netflix?

G: Of course we do. We are part of everything. Many times, we are behind the material, just as we are here with you. We may not be holding the camera or fleshing out the narrative, but more often than not, inspiration is offered.

L: So you might offer an inspired idea or thought, but you are not calling the shots and, therefore, are not the ones injecting violent scenes and images into them?

G: Sometimes in order to get our message across, one must look past the prose and pomp to reach the masses.

L: Then I should stop being so judgmental of those who consistently share images of violence and oppression, especially of women.

G: We would say it this way. One whose message is of love will find a way to infuse the material with shards of cynicism to wake the masses and lead them toward truth, as is the case of your franchise known as "Star Wars." Whenever one seeks profit, fear is the driving force behind the material, and it should, therefore, be consumed with caution.

L: Is it fairly obvious which is which? Because I think in Hollywood, most would be on the side of just doing things for profit and very few from a space of love. I tried to sell TV shows that were sharing a good message and got shot down time and time again.

G: Is it not hard to imagine in a society where 99 percent of you are living within the separation, that 99 percent of what you are viewing has a message not of God?

L: Yes, that makes sense. So most of what's out there is garbage born out of fear, picked and procured by fear-minded beings?

G: We might say it differently, but yes, there are those who seek only profit at the top of the food chain, so to speak, in your town of Hollywood.

L: Why do you sometimes speak backward?

G: The language with which you are most comfortable is not the only one we speak.

L: That has become quite obvious to me throughout this book. I am trying to teach my son about God, the Universe, and the nature of your thoughts creating your life. What is the best way to teach a child about all of this?

G: We will speak of this further in book two. Suffice it to say your calling has to do with shifting education away from philosophy-based learning to an assimilation-based modality. For this is why, within your experience, you have recognized both and the need for a change in many parts of your country.

L: We have moved away from letting kids just be kids to forcing them to learn too fast and grasp too-difficult concepts at too young of an age. I am not a teacher, so I can only speak as a parent, but yes, it frustrates me that the emphasis is more on academic endeavors than learning by doing and experiencing.

G: Through experience. Only when children experience something for themselves will true learning be had.

L: Often, though, we have to teach through words, and so for now what words can I use or suggest to him about how to handle everyday situations that arise out of frustration, bullying, racism, sexism, or other issues facing our nation and world, really?

G: Intention is powerful. Prayer is powerful. Breath is powerful.

L: Yes, I understand that, but I can't send my son off to school and have him stopping to pray every single second. The teachers and other kids might think he was a bit strange.

G: Do you not see that this is the pervasive problem in your entire world. Why cannot prayer be used at all times?

L: Because our world is our world right now, and to send my kid into it using "spiritual tools" is quite possibly going to make him the weird kid, and I do not wish for him to be the weird kid.

G: What's wrong with being the weird kid?

L: Nothing and everything. I want to teach him to stand up for himself and to take a step back, take a deep breath, and not let situations get the best of him. I want to teach him to be cautious on a playground and leery of someone's intentions. I want to make sure if someone is mean to him, he doesn't internalize it but also knows how to fight back against a bully. I want to teach him to stand up for what he believes in and yet also be aware of the words that may cause him harm.

G: All of it. All of those things are perfection. Teach him all of it or none of it. It does not matter. What matters is that he experiences those things for himself. Those ideals that serve him and those ideals that do not serve him. He must, however, learn this himself. For it is when we impose our ideals on our children that many times, if not most, they are lost to an unforgiving world. Let him learn exactly as you have spoken that you wish all children to learn, through experiences.

L: I completely get that. However, what do I say when he is frustrated and lashing out? What do I do when he doesn't want to clean his room and talks back to me? How do I get

him to appreciate what he has in life and stop asking for a toy every two seconds?

G: Those are, and you will not like to hear this—

L: Learned behaviors?

G: Exactly. He learned through experience that toys are rewards not punishments. Give. Get. Receive. He lashes out because it has been done for him his whole life, and he has not yet experienced that he must do for himself. Frustrations lie within all children who are not allowed to speak and be that which they want to be. Children want to express themselves as much as adults do, but they normally don't get to, do they? They are told where to go, what to do, and how to act or behave and to sit still and be quiet. "Children should be seen and not heard," your elders would say. Yet this is not accurate representation of what is really going on here. Children should be heard, period. When a child speaks, listen and engage. Don't stop the energetic flow. Let him or her speak and speak freely. You may learn something yourself.

L: That's a beautiful sentiment, but you try telling an irate six-year-old to calm down, and you'll see what happens.

G: We see what happens. The angrier he gets, the angrier a parent gets. The angry parent begets the angry child, and thus, a cycle is performed again and again.

L: So how do we stop that?

G: Listen. Receive. Respect.

L: What does that mean?

G: Listen to their request. Receive the message. Respect their wishes.

L: That is not always possible. If I say to my son we are going to the grocery store because I need to get food and he screams and hollers because he wants to stay home, respecting his wishes is just giving into him, and I don't think that's good either.

G: Respect their wishes. That does not mean you always give into demands. It means you respect and understand their point of view. Let us give you an example here.

"Son we need to go to the grocery store now to get some food."

"But Mom, I don't want to go right now!"

You all would say, "I don't care what you want, we are going and that is that. If we don't go now we will starve!" or some overly exaggerated musing. The son would then get angrier and angrier until it escalates into some type of negotiation or punishment.

L: That sounds about right. So if God were the parent, how would God handle this situation?

G: "Son, it is time to go to the grocery store so that we may get some food for dinner."

"But I don't want to go right now!" he would argue.

We would say, "And I am understanding this may be a disruption for you. However, a short trip is right and necessary."

"But I don't want to go!" he would yell.

We would say, "Not wanting to go is a natural reaction to being interrupted while you are playing and having fun. We understand this and apologize and promise we will be back as quickly as possible."

Listen. Receive. Respect.

L: Well, I will try it your way and see what happens.

G: We are not proposing this is the right way or even one that will lead to the certain outcome. We are simply showing you a different approach.

L: And what of trying to teach my son about turning inward for advice and asking for divine guidance?

G: You are doing this already, and it is a job well done. Again, we will tackle much, if not all, of this in our next book.

L: Earlier you used a phrase to describe Adam and Eve at the time of "supplementative creation," and I didn't quite understand it. But today while I listened to *Conversations with God, Book Three*[20], you talked about other civilizations, which destroyed themselves, existing before our current earthly one did. So does that word "supplementative" mean what I think it does?

G: Yep, it sure does. Adam and Eve are the beginning of your current world's earthly story, but it in no way reflects the entire story. To supplement is to add to something else, and so we now ask you to understand this truth—before this was something else, an entire world created by me, for me, for you all to enjoy. And you did, for a long, long time, until you didn't. Destruction rained upon your society (and I say your because you all were there too, still are, as everything that has ever happened and will ever happen exists always). You blew it up, accidentally, of course.

L: We blew it up?!

G: Yes. Your technological advances far outweighed your spiritual advances, and so it went kaboom, an entire civilization wiped out by greed and power and madness.

L: And we just began again?

G: I like how you said "we" instead of asking if God created another civilization. You are learning. Yes. We created again, as we will always. Life is a never-ending process of creation. You are born again. You will try again. You may fail again. Or not. You will all decide your country's fate.

L: You said country and not planet. Are you referring to our current presidential issue or our nuclear problems with North Korea?

G: I am. Your current problem is one of significant importance right now.

L: Could our entire nation be wiped out?

G: Well, not wiped out, but atomic bombs have destroyed entire nations before; imagine what a nuclear bomb would do. Your country would be demolished and your planetary evolution changed forever.

L: Why would someone do this? How is this even possible?

G: Ask that of your leaders who bombed Japan.

L: But I feel as if we have evolved beyond that? Have we not?

G: You have not. This is not to say you haven't evolved in a multitude of ways, but come on now, what really has changed since World War II? World War III is upon us, and righteous be the few who wish to harm the many.

L: So what do we do?

G: Do not sit idly by, any of you. For if you wish to change, then change. Accept glory. Proclaim God and the Universe (or whatever term you use) is our source, our protector, our guidance system. Think not of what may happen but what will happen, a resolution for all. Inner peace shall set you all free.

L: Well, what happens if that doesn't occur and Kim Jong Un blows us all up?

G: Then the evolutionary process begins again. But wouldn't it be better to live out this lifetime?

L: Um, hell yes. Excuse my language.

G: There is no hell, but we understand the use of your term here. Remember that any thought that stems from fear is an illusion. So perhaps the world would cease to exist, but you all would just return back to Love. Problem solved. No biggie.

L: No biggie?! Sorry, I don't see it that way.

G: We know you don't, but you will. Your divine natures require it.

L: What do you mean by that?

G: The essence of your soul is aligned with higher truths. Higher truths are being revealed to you now at a rapid pace, in rapid succession. Your journey is nearly complete from a spiritual perspective, not a death perspective, as you were just thinking.

I lost the voice within for a minute.

G: Do you see how fear stops the flow of information?

L: I do! When you made that statement, I went into a panic for a second.

G: We know.

L: And when I was there, I stopped hearing your words.

G: Precisely. Energy vibration is diminished whenever fear is present. Fear stops the flow.

L: I wish I were better at typing.

G: Us too.

L: It's so hard to type as fast as you talk.

G: We can help with this.

L: How?

G: "Dear God, as we are cocreating this material, please slow down your words so that we may create in a more cautious manor and words do not get lost."

L: Oh my god. As you said that, I heard you say it in a slower manner! That is crazy.

G: It is not crazy at all. It is truth. Shall we find a happy medium between fast and slow?

L: Yes. The other way was too slow.

G: We know. It was done to prove a point that you are indeed talking to "God."

L: OK, good. I am glad you brought this up because it leads into a question I wanted to ask. Recently I have been reminded through a friend who has no religious affiliation that the word God and prayer can be very off putting for some as it was for me for so long. How can I better describe to someone who does not necessarily believe in God (or prayer) that what we are speaking is truth? Or at the very least, can we

replace the words with something less teeming with religious undertones?

G: Too many questions at once. Let's take one at a time. First, call me anything you want. I am not a word or a thing. I just am.

L: I Am.

G: Right. So whatever word (we have covered this before) works for you works for me.

L: But how can we pray without asking God to help us?

G: God is doing unto as you do unto yourself. Therefore, there is no need to pray for anything except what it is that you desire for yourself and your evolutionary process.

L: But when we prayed here, many times you started with "Dear God."

G: Not always, but yes. We do this because it is necessary for some to hear it this way or read it. It is what they believe in, and belief as you know is very, very powerful. Belief in God is not necessary to pray. Prayer begets bargaining begets constitution of creationism.

L: What does that mean?

G: The only way to truly have what it is you desire is to proclaim for yourself that you already have it, which, of course, you do from a spiritual standpoint.

L: Give me an example. I want to finish this book and have it be a best seller. How would I pray on this without using the name God in the asking?

G: Proclaiming, not asking.

L: Right. OK, hit me with it.

G: "Oh, Father of all life."

L: Still implies God.

G: So what?

L: I want it for those who do not wish to pray to a godlike figure.

G: They must in some way believe in the God concept in whatever form they wish to express it.

L: So let's try again.

G: "Oh, heavenly Force of energy."

L: Better. One last try. Please.

G: "All of the universe, let us come together to proclaim we are expanding our horizons and enlightening those who wish to come forward and remember spiritual truths. As we create our books and material, let those who are ready come to us so that we may create the experiences of love, joy, and happiness. Amen."

L: Do we have to say Amen?

G: No, but it's nice. It's like an exclamation point at the end of a sentence to really give it some oomph! See what I mean?

L: Yes! OK, lastly for tonight. What about the word prayer?

G: What about it? It's a great word. One of my, of our, favorites.

L: But not a word everyone can thoroughly get behind. Can you give us a word that doesn't have religious undertones?

G: Controlled emotion. Focused intention. Pejorative proaction. Putting the cart before the horse.

L: Putting the cart before the horse?

G: If you put the cart before the horse, you are proclaiming you want what is already ahead of you. Isn't that what you are asking for in your focused intention?

L: Indeed. How about one word here to replace prayer?

G: Protection.

L: Protection?

G: You asked for one word. To be protected is to pronounce that guidance from the Universe is necessary to keep from harm's way. The only true harm is the one you make up. God's protection is almighty. Amen.

L: I think we will just go with prayer.

G: I think that's best, but I, again, do not care nor judge. Whatever works for you works for me.

L: Can we go back to pejorative proaction? When I looked up the word pejorative it does not seem to apply here to prayer.

G: And why is that?

L: Pejorative means disapproving or negatively thinking about a group. Proactive means to act in anticipation of future things occurring. How is pejorative proaction prayer?

G: Prayer is a talking to God through your actions and words. Your words coupled with your actions create your experiences. When you create from a space of individuality, one that is separate from God or the Creator or Universe (again we care not what you call it), you create wildly or insufficiently. Whenever you cocreate and commune with the spirit, which guides and protects you, that which is negative is negated in so that you are pejoratively (disapprovingly) reacting to your proaction (attempt to create alone to ward off a negative experience), and thus, a prayer of replacement is undertaken to swap the aloneness for the oneness.

L: I guess that explains it well enough.

G: Many concepts will be hard to grasp here, and as you write, so shall you learn. We have a vaster knowledge of words than one can even comprehend.

L: Tell me about dreams.

G: What would you like to know?

L: What is their purpose? Why do we have them?

G: Dreams come from intuition or intuitive notions.

L: Do we dream of past, excuse me, simultaneous lives?

G: Yes.

L: Can we spend time with our departed loved ones there?

G: Yes. You are answering your own questions here really because you already know the answers here, but I will indulge you in one more.

L: Do our dreams offer warnings about future events or illusions to come?

G: Yes.

L: How? And why?

G: How is easy. You dream them. Your mind creates them for you. Why is much more complicated to explain here. However, we will try to satisfy your curiosity even though you already know the answer within.

L: Well, please indulge me, all of you.

G: That is so good. You truly are learning, and for this we are truly proud. Both your dad and brother would be proud, were they able to be with you in human form again.

L: I thought they were always with me.

G: In spirit form, yes. All minds are interconnected and one.

L: They would only be proud of me in human form, not as a spirit?

G: Of course not; in spirit form you would have no need of such an emotion as we are all one whole being. We are no longer separate. Pride is a human (and other culture) concept.

L: Got it. Back to dreams, then. Why do our dreams predict for us future events?

G: One must first be reminded (or know) all events are happening simultaneously, that is to say all at once. Each lifetime's occurrences though are created from a multitude of possible outcomes. Therefore, it is possible in your worlds to "mess up" or miscreate, which would be more accurate of a universal term. Everything you have ever been or ever will be has already taken place. Yet your free will choices make the ending or possibility unknown for you. You have a multitude of outcomes available unto your experience. "Possibilities are endless" again is not an accurate phrase. "Possibilities are expressed" would be more accurate in the theology of the universe. If you go left, you may encounter love; if you go right, you may encounter fear. Left, love. Right, fear. We will explain it this way in simple terms you all may understand here. Left. Right. Left is where love choices lie, and so the outcome may be positive and joyful, albeit not always the choicest destination one would have expected. If you go right, you nose-dive into fear, and fear will create a circumstance you will then need to deliver yourself out of, and the game then continues. The next choice will have the same effect. Left, love. Right, fear. The choice is yours. The outcome is which choice you choose. They both exist for you at all times. This is why we always have taught to think from a space of love. For this produces a much more pleasant experience for humans and other species upon other planets and places.

L: Whoa. I still am shocked every time I hear that. But back to dreams, how can they predict—

G: Not predict. Pre-dictate.

L: OK, pre-dictate our future. I asked if they were warnings, and you said yes.

G: They are warnings. Warnings for you to watch what it is you are thinking about in the current time-space continuum of your experience as a human. Shall we look at one of your dreams we know you can recall?

L: Sure.

G: Once you had a dream sequence where you were speaking in front of an audience. At once was the audience awaiting your speech. As you became ready to begin, a large scaffolding, we shall call it, was placed in front of you, and you were unable to begin. As the mechanism was waiting to be removed, your audience began to dwindle and disappear, and you found yourself alone, unable to give your speech.

L: Yes. I remember it well, and I took it to mean that I was feeling unheard by my boss at *Access Hollywood* and other people who did not hire me from other shows.

G: Correct. Your message was correct, that you were feeling unheard. Your larger warning was to decide whether to remove that scaffolding yourself and continue on or let it drown you out and dim your light. Which did you do?

L: I dimmed my light. I stopped really pursuing the on-camera stuff.

G: Precisely. And what happened?

L: I became disillusioned, and that may have been around the time I left *Access Hollywood.*

G: It was, yes. However, had you heeded that warning, your outcome could have been different. You went right into fear. You created the possibility from fear, and, therefore, not only did you leave the job but you were never able to return to the spotlight, so to speak. Your other option was to go left, to love yourself enough to know that you are capable of anything; and what does it matter who hears or sees you? Move the scaffolding, share the message.

L: And if I had done that, which obviously I didn't, what outcome was possible for me?

G: Another year of *Access Hollywood* growing your brand and creating more unique opportunities for yourself.

L: Even if I had done that, would I have left anyway?

G: Not necessarily. Remember you have free will always. You may have, however, returned to your frustrated self and indulged nonsensical expectations and created, then again, a situation where you wanted to leave. Or you may have become the greatest interviewer of all time interviewing the greatest being of all time! Oh, wait. You are already doing that now. So, you see, my dear, all roads eventually will lead back to where you are meant to be, which is you, body-mind-spirit you; you are meant to be wholly perfect and pure love.

L: Was there no chance of me not writing this book?

G: Not necessarily. Again, you will always have free will. You will always have the choice to denigrate yourself into fear; meaning to allow the ego to attack a soul's true nature. Life is a never-ending process of creation with multiple outcomes based on the actions of love or fear. Right or Left. You choose. You decide. You create.

L: Does that mean, then, there are only two outcomes? The one from love and the one from fear, not a multitude of outcomes for each and every choice?

G: Yes. Love. Fear. The choice is yours. The outcome is yours.

L: So was there no chance of me ever being a well-respected, famous TV host like an Oprah Winfrey?

G: We did not say or imply that. If every choice you made focused on the left, the love side of life, you may have very well ended up being what it is you (the ego you) wanted to be.

L: But I would not have ended up here writing this book, then?

G: Why would you say that? Look at Oprah, the *Super Soul Sunday* sharer of love and universal truths. Her path to righteous world truths led her to exactly where she is. Do you not think you could have come to this place on another train? The L train straight from Love station. You absolutely could have. You would be sitting in your dressing room one day, like she was, wondering what all this madness in the world is really about and how to enact change, and you too (the you who chose love in every circumstance) could be writing this exact book with this exact message. Though the questions may not be exactly the same, the message would be. For the message of the Universe, of God, of Spirit, has and never will change. You are all beautiful creatures of the universe capable of creating in and of the likeness of me, of us, of all of us.

L: Well, how do we tap into the dream and not interpret the message wrongly?

G: "Dear God, this morning I awoke from a beautiful dream, an important message from God, Spirit, and the angels. May I not interpret this dream wildly inaccurately as my ego often does. May you please, may we please, interpret and understand the dream's message appropriately so I may learn and grow and choose love always, each and every time. Amen."

L: We have so many choices every single day of our lives. That is a lot of information for the Universe to hold for us.

G: Indeed. It is. You have no idea the magnitude of what you all will return to one day. In your remembering will you be saved.

L: It's so much to take in.

G: It is. We shall stop here for now if you want. You have the choice. You want to ask another question about this concept, but you already know the answer. First thought is always the right thought.

L: Yes. So this means that in love relationships there are always two possible outcomes? If we choose love, we may wind up staying with a partner. If we choose fear, that partnership would end or be a total mess?

G: Yes, in so much that the partner you have drawn to yourself also has two choices in every matter as well. It's too complicated for human minds to grasp. So to explain it here might be difficult. Your soul knows this answer, and you may have a think of it and get back to us.

L: I will because you said earlier we are all soulmates.

G: That you are.

L: I am confused how this would all work because this notion would make it seem we would only ever have a couple of partnership outcomes. Yet I have had so many.

G: You have. You have chosen fear every single time, and so you have created a multitude of possible partners as have they. Remember, we all cocreate together, so their possibilities are mixed together with your possibilities, and simple multiplication would explain how it is possible to have millions of potential soul partners, as you have called it. Let us take the example of someone who has been married to her high school sweetheart. She has chosen to swipe left for love. (Your dating apps have it backward, you know.) In each moment she chooses love of that partner, she shall stay with that partner. When one chooses to denigrate into fear via the ego, they then have the possibility of no love coming into their lives or a new love coming into their lives. So there are in fact two possibilities for them. If they stay in fear, they will stay loveless until such time they choose love again. If they choose love, they may in fact find a new partner almost immediately. That partner may then choose whether he wants to view the relationship with love or fear. If the partner chooses love, a possibility exists where they may cocreate as soulmates again. If the partner chooses fear, another possible set of outcomes comes into play.

L: So it is possible to have multiple outcomes?

G: Every outcome is either of love or fear. So it is inaccurate to say there are multiple outcomes. What is more accurate to say is there are multiple outcomes possible from choices made by each individual soul's choices and the choices of the partner's individual soul as it relates to the topic of relationships. In any circumstances are you able to create a multitude of possible outcomes, but outcomes are always from the dual nature: Love versus Fear.

L: Let me ask it this way, since I am not understanding and

feel as if you are saying two different things here. On one hand, it seems you are saying there are only two outcomes for each choice. On the other hand, it seems you are saying there are multiple outcomes.

G: Possibilities.

L: What is the difference?

G: Outcomes equals end results. Possibilities, of which you have many (based on choices of love or fear), equals multiple results but not end results. Outcomes are always the same. Either you return to love or you "die" of fear. Possibilities are endless but are not the end; only the outcome is the end. The game does not end until it is over. You have multiple choices to play the game, but the result is always the same. When the game ends, the end of the game is the outcome. The game will ultimately end. Either you get there as a champion, having mastered all the moves and levels until it is over, or you mess up the game and it ends. Sometimes the game ends early. Sometimes you almost make it to the end as a winner. Sometimes you get past certain levels and are ecstatic, only to be kicked in the gut when you got so far but still lost the game. However, in the end, no matter what the choices, the game will be over. You will either be ecstatic or exasperated. Along the way, you might have moments of exhilaration or moments of exasperation depending on the choices you made during the game. Either way, the game is over; the outcome is the end result. All of life is this dance. It is the cha-cha. 1-2-3. 1-2-3.

L: Um, yeah that is a very exhausting to understand.

G: Exhausting or frustrating?

L: Frustrating. That is a better word, yes. It is frustrating because I don't understand it that well. I mean, I sort of get it, but I sort of don't. It's one of those things I will have to read over and over again.

G: Let us take the example of Oprah Winfrey we spoke of earlier. Her choices have led her to the outcome of her being at one with the Universe, which is our goal for all of you in human form. Her end result is enlightenment, which she has obtained. She is *awake.* Her choices have led her there. However, had she chosen to stay at her show and be dragged into fear, more likely than not, she may either still be on the air or sharing stories of degradation and images of fear with her audience even to this day. This possibility existed. Yet this is not what happened, as you know. She has practiced and preached, prayed and promised to enlighten others, and therefore, her outcome (end result) is enlightenment. Her only two outcomes were Love (enlightenment) or Fear ("death"). All have many possibilities when it comes to how death comes about. However, for all, that is the end result until reunification with God or Source Energy or whatever name you want to call it.

L: So is this why you said there are only two outcomes?

G: Yes. End results would be a better phrase, and perhaps from this is where your misinterpretation came. Multiple possibilities. Only two outcomes from the dual nature of love versus fear. Are you understanding better now?

L: I think so. Just to wrap up what question we initially began with here. We should really pay attention to our dreams and when we don't understand, ask for guidance and explanation?

G: Yes. Always, we would add here. Always ask for guidance

when undertaking dream interpretation or any interpretation of something that we have sent in the form of a message or sign. Remember, it is always best to cocreate. It would suffice to ask, "Is this accurate?" as well if one's own interpretation is undertaken.

L: And we will get the answer or a yes or no?

G: Always will you be answered.

L: Even knowing all I know and being able to commune here and get answers from you, I still have some really terrible days. There are still work stresses and life stresses that are near impossible to shake off. What can we do to shake the human off of us?

G: Why would you want to do that? You should do no such thing. To be human is divine, just as to be spirit is divine. You are learning and growing and receiving, and therefore, all experiences, terrible or not, are of value. What is of no value here is for you to beat yourself up on those bad days or even bad moments. What is upon you is to practice vibration, vibrating a different energy whenever possible so we may transform the moments.

L: And how do we do that?

G: Give me a moment, a minute. Even sixty seconds of intense breathing would ideally change the topic inside your mind that is giving you so much trouble, be it stress or work troubles or dinner table topics such as your world events. One need only practice mindful meditation at any given time, and I am there. I am always there.

L: It's so hard to remind ourselves to do that though. We get caught up so much in the daily grind. Today was yet another terrible day where the stress of work and living up to other people's expectations and fears, doubts, and worries came back in full force. It's in those moments where I remember I am human. It's easy to sit here and tell people to turn to God in moments of grace and ease. However, most of the world is living in stress and anger and frustration. I have been very much reminded this week of that. How can I teach others to turn to God when I am in the thick of struggle and strife myself? How can I prove all of this is real and true and that we can cocreate with God or the Universal Presence when I can barely get my own life together? I am angry and grouchy dealing with the everyday stresses of work—bosses, deadlines, people not emailing me back, and not feeling respected in my career. I am not a spiritual warrior right now. I am a spiritual flop.

G: Are you done?

L: Yes. I think so.

G: There's more.

L: Just a little bit more. What on earth can one do when faced with the massive burden of being human?

G: Now that's a question worth undertaking. To be human is no such thing as a burden.

L: First may we pray here? I feel I need to strengthen my

connection and lose the ego voice so that the words are correct.

G: Go ahead.

L: "Dear God, please help me understand how to release the heavy burdens of our human existence. Show the path to least resistance to follow my heart's desires and not my head's anguish as we cocreate this material together. Release any and all writings that do not serve the highest good of all who would undertake the notion to read the musings of what seems to be a mad woman, but who is actually a master in the making. For only she knows the truth within, that we are all one. One light. One heart. One soul. One power. Amen."

G: Very good.

L: You wrote that.

G: We wrote that together. *You* and *I* equals *We*. Now there is a good book title. You and I = We.

L: Seems too easy.

G: You do know we will together create the perfect title for this book.

L: I hope so.

G: You know so.

L: I know so.

G: We have missed you.

L: Where have I been?

G: Down in the dumps. Feeling sorry for yourself. Acting selfishly but in a way that no longer serves who you truly are now.

L: Which is what?

G: A soul being a human rather than a human being a soul.

L: Meaning what?

G: A soul being a human knows the truth: that it is a divine being of light and love. Nothing, truly nothing real can be threatened and nothing unreal exists. Therefore, you are (and you know you are) capable of anything. Anything that you wish to create can be yours for the taking (so to speak) when you simply wish upon a star, and that star is you and me and we.

L: Wish, not want.

G: Wishing and hoping and dreaming of better tomorrows is merely an ego's foolish belief in separation. Wanting is no more than reminding yourself of that which you do not already have. A wish of cocreation sets in motion that which is rightfully already yours.

L: But you said, "Anything that you wish to create can be yours," so that seems to contradict you saying that wishing "is merely an ego's foolish belief in separation."

G: And we are glad you asked. Here now we shall clarify. You see all "wishes" have already been fulfilled from a godly perspective. You can't wish for what already exists, because what you wish for does exist as possibility in the field of potentiality. A wish of cocreation is reminding oneself that which exists already is attainable more quickly by returning to the presence of the One.

L: So rather than wish for a result to appear, we should instead wish for, or return our thoughts back to, our oneness?

G: Exactly.

L: And what would one say to do that?

G: "Oh, heavenly Father, I cannot know what it is I wish to remember as factual evidence of my divineness. Show me, show we, how our oneness makes manifest all that is desired from the earthly plane of existence. For in the kingdom of heaven have we no need of material possessions. It is only in the earthly realm where possessions are a necessity, and rightly I shall own anything that is of my highest good, my highest potential for growth and evolvement. Those items all of us desire here shall include clothing, food, natural resources of water and sunlight and air, and all manner of joyful celebration. We shall never fear our resources running out nor fear our financial burdens tearing us asunder. For we know our abundance comes in many forms—abundance of love, laughter, and light. Amen."

L: Asunder? What do you mean "nor fear our financial burdens tearing us asunder"?

G: Your lack of finances shall never strip you of the knowledge of your oneness with the Universe. You shall always remember the bank and trust of God A. Mighty is open and ready to receive and return.

L: Interesting how you said you are open to "receive and return" rather than to just give us money.

G: We would never say that because, as we have said many times before here and in many forms of communications (books, DVDs, CDs, downloads), in order to receive, you must first give. Nothing comes from that which is not first given to another. We cannot take that which you are not willing to give—be it your bad attitude or lack of finances or any insane notion of the human mind's ego thoughts. We can only give that which you are willing to get by way of giving. "Give me your tired, your poor, your huddled masses yearning to breathe free . . ." The same goes here for all of you. Give us your anger, your resentment, your pain, your triumph, and your tragedy. Give us your poorness, your pompous behavior, and your perfectly imperfect scenarios, and may all be transformed instantaneously because they are not real. Truly are they imaginings of the ego mind. Fear is ego. Love is heart, soul, and Spirit together making manifest what desires you truly have. No one desires misfortune or fortitude, for you have no needs for those. You only need be mentally capable of handling such dire circumstances of your earthly world when you feel you have lost your way. Losing one's way is a grand illusion. You are never lost but only found in all our loving arms. We await your words reminding yourself, "I have no need for these illusion-based thoughts. I have only a need of my oneness with the All That Is."

L: Thank you for your words, truly, thank you but this is a difficult process for me. Why? Why is it so hard to live that

way? Why do I keep falling back into the same old cyclical patterns?

G: Because, my dear, as we had stated early, you are in fact human and in a body. Your goal in being human was growth of soul and to evolve one's being to the next level of consciousness. This is not done in one day's work or one year's work or even in one lifetime's work. This is done gradually, over time. Practice makes perfect, but you will be practicing for a long, long time to come. So we will say this to you, to all of you. Do your best. Make your mistakes. Be human, but also be Spirit. It is possible to do both. Whenever possible, turn to us, to the we that is God and the Universe. Remind yourself of what is possible in this current lifetime that you have chosen to incarnate into. Remind yourself. Say, "I am capable of cocreating with the Universe. Together, may our bond be remembered in any instant." Then go about your daily life, and live it. Feel it fully. When it hurts, feel it. When it raises you up to a level of joyousness, feel that fully. Whenever illness or ailment strikes, take the pill, see the doctor, nurse the wounds, and relieve the pain, but also remind yourself of God's plan for all of you, which is not sickness but health, perfect health for mind, body, and soul. Turn inward and say, "This notion of sickness may feel very real to me though I know it to be illusory, and therefore, I shall not fall victim to its unrealness. Instead, I shall return to my cocreator and declare I am healthy, we are healthy, and this suffering shall be healed. Amen."

L: Whoa. Your words never fail to shock me. Just when I am about to fall back into the trap of believing this perhaps is all my own writings do I realize I am not writing this alone. It may be my fingers typing, and I am hearing the words in my head, but the words are not mine; they are coming from

a different source. I hear you changing the voices to different ones right now.

G: We are, and we are doing this to show you that we are all one. We are literally millions upon billions of voices together as one cohesive collaborator. We may remind any and all who are reading or listening to (or perhaps one day watching) our words that any one of you is capable of cocreation and of the feat that Laura has undertaken. We have spoken to and through many a healer and will continue to do so throughout all of time and space. It is in our gratitude we express thanksgiving to all willing to undertake sharing our words without need for compensation (not to say this won't come or be a part of their experience, as for many it will) or fear of condemnation, which will come no matter how spiritual you think you are.

L: Well, I wouldn't say I have no fear of condemnation; I know it's not going to feel very good to be called crazy or blasphemous or said to be spreading voodoo gossip, but I guess in this internet age, we are all kind of used to it.

G: True. Your internet has become a place of mass condemnation rather than how it was originally intended, which was to be a way of sharing information quickly and efficiently. You humans have a way of destroying that which is indestructible.

L: That we do. I feel as if most of us mean well when we invent things, but when the masses get ahold of those things, the fear seeps out, and we begin to be judge and jury of each other.

G: That sounds like something we would say, minus the judgmental part of it.

L: Was I being judgmental about it?

G: Yes, but we do not judge for that; we simply observe. We always observe human behaviors with wonderment. One might say you are all quite predictable in nature.

L: That we are, my friend. That we are. If only we could change our behaviors, then I would imagine we would have a better world to live in.

G: Not necessarily. You would have to drastically change your behaviors to be more like God, each and every one of you, to even have a stone's chance of a better world. There is so much fear and judgment and lack of respect for your fellow man out there.

L: Sad but true. Why can't we all just get along? Why do we hate one another? Well, not me so much, but why do we judge and define ourselves and others as different and separate?

G: Because you are "of ego." For most of you, if not all, are being ruled by the ego, the fear mindset, which invades the soul, body, and spirit consciousness. "Lose the ego, lose the fight!" This is what the coach of a high school football team might tell his players in order to motivate them to succeed and beat the rival team. For this is how your world has operated since the dawn of time. Fight or flight. Sink or swim. Kill or be killed. For this is not of God. None of this is true. Only love is real, only goodness and kindness and forsaking of no one. We would coin the word "nothers" here. Forsaking of "no others" is how the real world, the only world that truly exists, operates.

L: But if we are here to grow and evolve and the process is slow, as you have said, then there is pretty much no way to make our world peaceful, kind, and loving.

G: We did not say that at all. It is entirely plausible and possible, we would add, to have a world filled with peace and love and kindness to all others. We are merely saying it would be difficult for all minds to join in mass consciousness, as all minds are in various stages of learning and remembering. It could be done, but it would take a massive undertaking by all thought leaders of the world, and we believe you are simply all not ready. This is not to say you may not all learn and grow and evolve through the tool of Love and not Fear. This is entirely available to all of you at all times (as we have stated so many times here).

L: What would happen if we all did wake up and remember all at once?

G: Your world would cease to exist as it is presently.

L: Like blow up?

G: Of course not, silly. You would merely all return to the loving space from which you all came.

L: What would become of Earth?

G: Nothing. It would still be there; it just would become a lonely planet. As you may know, there are many lonely planets.

L: Are you saying that on other planets at one time there were

civilizations that existed, which did evolve beyond and return to the universal energy?

G: Yes. And then they returned again to their planet and evolved again, and then they moved onto other planetary planes. Remember, we have said you are always learning and growing and evolving, and therefore, creation never ceases nor stops. It just keeps going and moving onto different places and spaces.

L: Have we landed on some of these planets?

G: Yes, your moon men have.

L: Then why have we not found artifacts proving this?

G: Perhaps you are not looking in the right place or perhaps your scientists and governmental secret agencies have decided it is best kept secret.

L: Somehow, I think it's—

G: A combination of both.

L: Yes.

G: You would be right. Your government as it currently operates seeks to misinform and manage expectations so that those who are enlightened may not prove the existence of what you are calling God. For to prove all that we have written here would render your theologies of religion wrong. And that would spark an outrage of massive political and sociological upheaval that your world may not be ready for currently.

L: Wait. Are you saying that it's OK for the government to hide these things from our society?

G: We did not say whether it was wrong or right; we merely observe your race of humans (you are all just one race, you know, as we have explained) to be incapable of properly digesting this universal truth at the consciousness most of the world currently is at.

L: Sadly, you are right; I'm sure.

G: We know we are right.

Even though we had spoken here of the difficulties of being human, I still am struggling to practice what is being preached here. I put the computer down and get sucked into work frustrations while on a work trip in New York City.

L: I spent the week working at my other job, my non-writing-a-book-with-God-and-the-Universe job. Yet again I will say it is so hard being human.

G: Was it a bad week?

L: Not necessarily.

G: Then what is your complaint?

L: Not a complaint. Merely an observation.

G: We feel this is important to clarify.

L: Yes, I mean nothing truly terrible happened; it was more just stressful.

G: And did it not work itself all out for the most part?

L: It did, yes.

G: So why are we even discussing. Of course, we know why; but do you?

L: Well, I guess I would say I felt out of sorts, very disconnected from the Universe and unable—

G: Not unable, unwilling.

L: All right. I will give you that one. Not unable but unwilling to turn back to the Universe or God or the energy from which we all come.

G: Very good terminology. And this is the heart of your problem right there. Your unwillingness at any moment to stop for one simple minute to acknowledge your creator and the ability to cocreate a new experience. Anytime, literally anytime you undertake a radical shift in perception may you change directions, switch the channel, or create a new result. You have no need to suffer endlessly. Yet all of the all of you refuse to listen. Therefore, we must continue with this dialogue until you get this, you really get this. We are with all of you, always. There is no place where we are not. There is no way we are not. We are not just with you, we are you. We are the Universe. Me. We. You are all one. Therefore, we create everything, literally everything—every experience, every moment, every spectacular, magnificent planetary moment—*Two*-gether. There are two of us: *You* and *We*.

L: Why can't I get this? Why can't I stay awake?

G: Oh, you are awake. There is no difficulty in your awakeness. You already know the truth. Belief is not your problem. Your problem is quite simple in nature.

L: And what is that?

G: Stubborn refusal to stop dwelling upon that which is not real.

L: And what is that?

G: Are you sure you would like to hear this?

L: Not really. But go for it, and I will accept any words you say and will keep them as they are written even if they are embarrassing to me personally.

G: It is not our intention to embarrass you or anyone else. It is merely our intention to teach you so that you may unlearn all that you think you know and remember all that is truth.

L: I am ready. Lay it on me.

G: OK, here it goes. You are stubborn. You are too self-righteous. You are pompous. You are self-deprecating. You are scared. You are lonely. You are tired of waiting. You want everything instantaneously to appear. You are impatient. You are bored. You are frustrated. You are picky. You are perfect.

L: I'm perfect? After all the other things you said, why would you then call me perfect?

G: Because you are. You all are. Warts and all. Your imperfections are what make you human. They are why you are always "stuck," as you would say, in mediocrity as you have written with us here earlier. However, this does not mean that we do not empathize with that which is the human part of you. We do understand being human can be challenging, which is why we are always and forever here to lend a helping hand. When a child's homework is difficult and hard to understand, what would happen if the child, say, asked its parent or teacher for help?

L: We would give them the answer or help them.

G: Would the child do a happy dance all the time, or would his frustrations sometimes get the best of him and cause him to lash out?

L: Sometimes the child would get it, and sometimes he would get frustrated. But I think he would be happy for the help. I see where you are going here with this.

G: God is the ultimate homework helper. However, what happens if students do the work by themselves?

L: Sometimes they are able to do it themselves, and other times they can't. So either they ask for help or they get frustrated and angry and don't even want to deal with it. Yep, this sounds a lot like life to me.

G: It is. A perfect metaphor for all of life. There are many wonderful, wonderful metaphors for all of life surrounding you always. You just need examine them further to reveal their truth.

L: All right. I will try more on a consistent basis to turn to God and the Universe for help. I will say, "Dear God, I cannot know how to handle this particular situation, yet I know you do. Please may we undertake this together as a team, *Two-gether.*" Yet again, you wrote that!

G: We know.

L: So can we talk about some of the issues you wrote about me that are holding me back and dissect, no, dissolve them. Forget dissecting them. Let's just wipe the slate clean.

G: You remember the T-shirt we showed you at the gym the other day?

L: Yes. "365 new days. 365 new beginnings." I knew that was for me.

G: Of course it was. We are always guiding you, and you know this. We feel your intuitiveness whenever you get that we are with you. Let us dissect this phrase first. We would break it down even further by saying 365 new days, 2,460 new minutes, 86,400 new seconds in a day. 365, 2,460, 86,400 new beginnings. "All in a day's work" should be replaced by "all day, every day shall we work at it." Creation never stops; therefore, you shall never stop remembering and returning to Source in any instant. In any instant you are healed of illusory thoughts, which serve no thing but the ego's thing, which is a fear sandwich. Fear on top. Fear in the middle. Fear on the bottom. Hold the onions, pickles, and mayo.

L: Are you hungry? Does God eat? What does God eat?

G: Whatever you are eating. Whatever you are experiencing, so too am I.

L: No, but seriously. I thought about this the other day. When someone dies and returns back to Source, does that person require food?

G: Nourishment, yes. Food, no. Only a body requires fuel, or food, as you call it on your planet.

L: So when we are pure spirit, we don't eat anything? We don't need food?

G: Not in earthly terms, no.

L: Sorry. I digressed away from my own issues for a minute.

G: There is no need for an apology. We are here always to answer any and all questions you may have. Now may we return to your earlier notion of relinquishing any and all subconscious thoughts that no longer serve you. When one's notion of oneself is subservient to its greater good, one would ask consistently to have them revealed as we have done here. To know yourself as God, Universe, or Spirit knows you requires little to no imagination. Simply sit quietly in contemplation and ask, "Where am I holding onto fear?" Then it will be shown or revealed to you. Whenever said notion is undertaken, only can a process of undoing take place. Then may we look deep within to discover our subconscious truths.

L: I heard the word "unworthy."

G: Very good. You uncovered one of your subconscious lifelong problems.

L: Unworthiness. Yes, I would say that is true. I feel unworthy of sharing this material. I feel unworthy of being in front of the camera because I don't look a certain way. I feel unworthy of being healthy because of my dad and brother dying. I feel unworthy of motherhood again because of my age. I feel unworthy of happiness because I suck at being anything. I feel unworthy of love from a partner because I can't seem to hold onto the love very long.

G: Very good. Now let us work toward releasing unworthy thoughts. "Father of heaven, Creator of the universe and all who seek to know and experience it, forever have I held onto the fearful notion that I am unworthy. Unworthy of love, joy, happiness, abundance, visibility, respect, and reverement. Forever have I lost my way through the forest of life and refused to look for guidance within. Forever now will I cherish every precious moment of creation so that I may relinquish to the heavenly energy source any and all thoughts that do not serve our highest good. Forever may we be healed. Amen."

L: It's easy to say those things but hard to live up to them.

G: See, this is what you are not understanding. It is not upon you to live up to them but rather just to be them. Sit quietly and be. Be amazing. Be strong. Be bold. Be beautiful. Be a bartender. Be a ballerina. Be rich. Be poor. Be smart. Be single. Be a mom. Just be. Whoever you wish to be, whatever you want, you must first believe you may be it before you can actually be it. "You cannot get there from here" is how we would say to you, to all of you, to stop being yourself and start being you, all of you—every possible thing you could ever want to be. You must first see it in your mind and thoughts or else you will be, continue to be, what it is you are: selfish, spoiled, fat, thin, ugly, poor. That which you are is that which you have thought yourself to always be. You will always be that until you remind yourself, "I do not wish to be fat; I wish to be thin. I am thin. I am perfect," or "I do not wish to be poor. I wish to be abundant. I am abundant and capable of creating wealth in my experience."

L: When you say it, it sounds so simple, and I think this is where we all get so caught up in our problems. Affirmations, meditation, prayer and positive thinking; they're all well and good, but until we see the proof of the manifestation of our desires, we can't get there from here, as you say.

G: Humans always want instant gratification. That is human nature and why it is so hard to get there from where you currently are standing. It's as if you are wearing cement shoes all the time. And we would say to you, "Here is a shovel, dig yourself out." Yet would you take the shovel and stop going if you did not see results?

L: Probably not. I would imagine if we had the shovel we would just keep going because it would make sense that at some point, no matter how long it took, that shovel would eventually get us out of the cement.

G: Yet on a spiritual level you have not found yourself capable of this notion of keeping going despite not seeing the evidence, even though we know you have seen some, if not many, miracles take place in your life.

L: Yes, you are right. I guess it's easier to believe in a tangible tool, such as a shovel, rather than the intangible thing, like God or the Universe, which we cannot see or touch. So to us, this life seems real and not the illusion everyone always speaks of in the spiritual community. It doesn't feel this way to us at all. It all feels very, very heartachingly real at all times. So what are we to do when we can't reconcile this very realness we feel with this "airy fairy" idea of a universal energy source guiding our lives if we tap back into it.

G: And we know this. Do you think we do not know this is how it feels to you all?

L: I did not say that. I am sure you all know this. Yet it doesn't change the fact that when the baby is crying and won't sleep, your husband cheats on you, your car breaks down on the way to work, your brother dies at a young age, or you accidentally fall off a cliff while taking a selfie that it all feels very, very real.

G: Yet when the person who falls off that cliff wakes up and is back home in the loving energy of the Universe, instantly he or she will know the truth we are speaking of always.

L: Yes, but, yet again, tell that to parents or friends or coworkers who are now grieving that loss or the millions of

people who see a story on Facebook the next day and then fear they will do something equally as stupid.

G: FEAR: the collective consciousness's biggest enemy. Sharing is not caring.

L: I know that it is so detrimental to our psyche when those types of stories get shared. Yet this is what happens in our society on a consistent, regular basis, and that is why it is so hard to shut off the human drive and turn on the spiritual drive.

G: Yet if you did such a thing as to fire up the internal drive, then you could cocreate a better, more satisfying experience from a humanistic perspective.

L: Yet again I will ask if it really is that simple?

G: Try it. Take it for a test drive, and see what would happen. What do you have to lose? Set an intention that for thirty days you will practice mindful meditation where you will ask yourself these questions. First, who am I? Second, who are we? Third, where am I holding on to fear, and then how shall I release it to God or the Universe? Were you to undertake this daily practice, to listen and to ponder all of them, a radical shift would begin to take place whereby everything we have written here will begin to take shape in your life, and you will see the manifestations you have been wanting and desiring.

L: Well, what have I got to lose? I will give it a try.

G: Let's start right now, then.

L: Who am I?

G: You are a child of the Universe. You are pure Spirit. Pure intention set forth by us/we so that you may create who you are as you see fit.

L: Who are we?

G: We are your loving guides here to protect, honor, and serve all that you have imagined your life can and will be. We are here with you, for you, always and forever more.

L: Where am I holding onto fear and how shall I release it to God or the Universe?

G: It is not necessary to do anything. It is necessary that you be, just be. Do nothing. Be everything you wish to be. For that is our only true lesson we would teach so you may remember more quickly that you already are what it is you wish to be. So be it.

L: SO BE IT! I like that. Easier said than done. My god, it's hard to just be. Life is messy and hard and frustrating. It's kids pulling your strings, deadlines looming, neighbors arguing, and news feeds filled with hate and anger and fear. It's as if we can't catch a break, ever. No wonder our world is so messed up. We literally cannot get our acts together because we are so stuck in the—

G: Illusion. Yes. You are, but it does not have to be like this.

L: But it is.

G: It is now.

L: Yes, and the now is the main problem. It's near impossible to get unstuck and believe in the power of God and the Universe when all around us is the evidence that there actually may not be a God. What kind of God would allow the floods that ravaged Houston last week? What kind of God would—

G: You are not answering your own question you asked.

L: Where am I holding onto fear?

G: Yes. Where? Where are you holding onto fear?

L: Everywhere. I lack faith and trust in the process. But I think that's so common. We all lack faith and trust in a God. Most of us do anyway, certainly the large majority, save for our ministers, priests, nuns, and clergymen.

G: Not all of you. It is true most of you lack any amount of faith or trust in Source Energy, God, as you have chosen to call it. All of your sentient beings on your planet have not the will power or the wanton energy to expend hours, minutes, or seconds even contemplating what it is to be one with God. Being one with God is true for all of you, yet virtually no one, has yet delivered you from your willingness to believe in that which you are not. You are not alone; you are not separate from God, Universe, or Source, *EVER*. Not one of you is left to your own devices *EVER*.

L: But that is not what it feels like. It feels as if we are all alone in this world. When you are looking for a job and the phone doesn't ring, you are down to your last ten dollars and can't

afford to eat (much less pay your bills), or you have prayed and prayed for a baby to come, the love of your life to arrive, or for your child to not be sick and nothing is happening, it feels as if we are in this world all by ourselves struggling to get by. This world sometimes feels like hell.

G: Because you have made it this way. It is not like this in other "worlds," as you would call it. In fact, it is quite the opposite. In other worlds, bills do get paid easily and on time because there is always enough, if you believe it to be true. Children and adults do heal, if they even get sick in the first place. Jobs are plentiful, and people do what it is they love or are passionate about, where they want, when they want, and with whom they want because they believe they can, and so they do. Worlds of wonderment exist in other places and spaces, and yet, though you all know this, you deny this. You deny God. You deny life on other planets. You deny time and space do not exist as you have created them on earth. You deny your right to cocreate. Deny. Deny. Deny. Your world works the way it does because it does not believe. Anyone asking the question (and we are glad you did) "Why would God do such a thing?" does not know God. You believe in the existence of a God. Yet no mere mortal can he be who smites the damned and raises the dead. This is no truth of God.

L: It isn't? I mean, I have never really thought that, but I guess most people do?

G: Most people do indeed. For you are closer to the truth (as many others have yet to remember their truth), but you too, even as we write this book together, do not believe in God or Universe or Source or whatever you would call us.

L: I would say that is still fairly accurate, yes. It's going back

to my original point that our lives are so filled with chaos; it's impossible to believe in a God granting wishes and wonderment.

G: Wonder not, for upon you are we about to unlock the greatest mysteries of life. You are all God. All of it.

L: Yes, I get that concept. You have said this before through other spiritual channels and teachers, and yet I still find it hard to imagine. If I am God, and my son, my friend, and my coworkers are all God, then shouldn't we be living the most amazing lives? Shouldn't we all be rich and famous if we want to be? Shouldn't we be capable of creating amazing lives for ourselves without all the hassle and drama and negativity surrounding us each and every day? How on earth can we all be God?

G: How on earth? You have come to the largest issue facing your planet. How on earth can any of you know God and that you are of God and part of God and Gods and Goddesses yourself?

L: Yes, how? If we could fix this "how," perhaps we could get to the knowing, and maybe, just maybe, things would change.

G: How can you not know? Mountains. Streams. Oceans. Rivers. Street lights. Street lamps. Facebook. iPads. Computers. Trees. Paper. Corn. Rice. Shall I go on?

L: I think I see your point. We have created all of this.

G: Not created. Cocreated. We all have made the all of everything. Everything that ever was and ever will be created has been created by you, all of you, in cocreation with—

L: God or the Universe, because we are all one. Again, I get this. I have heard this over and over and over. We are all one. There is only one of us here, but it does not explain the larger issue at hand. If we are all God, and that is a big if, then why are we each individually creating crappy lives for ourselves?

G: *BE*cause you are not in cocreation (most of the time); you are in re-creation, re-creating moments from your pasts, pasts that you have not yet remembered, and you are, therefore, stuck in cycles of miscreation. *BE*cause. Be the cause of your experience not the effect of it. Misaligned thoughts. Miscreation.

L: Can you tell me some misaligned thoughts?

G: I am not good enough. I am not worthy. I am ugly. I am fat. I am not a good person. I am horrible and disfigured. I am incapable of keeping or finding a job. I am unlovable. I am imperfect, broken, and shattered. I am no longer able to believe in a God because I see no evidence of its existence in my life and the lives of others near, far from, and around me.

L: We do think like that, most of us, don't we?

G: Yes. You do. All of you at some point in a day, in an hour, in an instant think these and many other thoughts that serve no one but an ego, which seeks to harm and inflict pain, suffering, and all of the "messes" from which you all believe you can suffer. But I am here to tell you there is a God (or Source or energy of the universe) from which you all came and of which you all are. Together may we live in peace and harmony. Apart we grow weary and "die." Together may we choose. Apart we lack. Together may we share in the joy and wonderment of all that life has to offer. Apart we suffer at the hands of a storm, a bow and arrow, a gun's bullet, a mother's wrath, or a neighbor's vengeance.

L: I feel as if you are also saying that when we suffer, you suffer too?

G: Well, of course. This would be true. When you suffer, I suffer. When you have pain, I have pain. Does it not make sense that if we are all one, we all suffer together the good and the bad of it all?

L: I guess, yes.

G: No. You know. You just don't remember right now, but you will. You all will someday.

L: I just don't get this, though. How can a God suffer? God is the almighty being, the Supreme Being.

G: So you do believe in a God?

L: I never said I didn't, just that I wasn't truly sure.

G: And now.

L: I am still not truly sure even as we write this. However, as I write the word "we," it does feel more and more true. As I write more and go back and read this material, I think it's fairly clear that I am not writing this as Laura, the separate being, because Laura, the individual, cannot write this well with this much clarity or write sentences and points that

make perfect sense. This independent Laura wishes I could write as quickly and succinctly as we are doing here because this Laura has never undertaken such an endeavor with such incredible ease. It feels as if someone else is talking in a quiet voiceless voice to me. It feels as if my fingers are just typing the ideas and thoughts I am hearing rather than typing my own thoughts, words, and feelings. So yes, at times I do believe in a God and the "we are all God" concept. But then something happens with work or my son or my mom or a friend, and I get sucked back into—

G: The illusion. All of life is this illusion.

L: And yet again you say that, but I don't quite understand it because it does not feel like an illusion. It all feels very, very real. And this is why we, as a collective consciousness, cannot get to the point where we believe 100 percent in a God or that we are all of God or part of God. The illusion feels too real. My headache right now tells me so.

G: And so you have yet again answered your own question of why your lives don't work the way you all want them to with grace and ease. Until all understand that all of life is a grand illusion of epic proportions, life on earth and other simultaneous lives you are living cannot and will not know God. For to know God would be to return to and with God. We would be together again, and we would rejoice in the knowing. Together we would feel the feelings of being separate and apart, as each of you now feels. Together we would raise our vibration and feel our Love's presence in all things. Together we would cocreate all of it together—joy and pain, happiness and sadness, love and loss, death and dying. To know God is to know yourself as God does—all of you—every nook and cranny, every delicious morsel.

To answer your larger question of God feeling the effects of what you are all creating—absolutely I feel your aches and pains, just as I feel your triumphs, your tragedies and tribulations, and your insane notions of grandiosity from which you all suffer. Your ups and downs are my ups and downs. Your victories are my victories. Together we all rise. Together we all fall. We are the Universe and all its magic and mysteries. We are all of it together.

L: So because we are all one, then you do feel what we feel? You do experience our tragedies?

G: Yes, and triumphs as I have said. Let's think about it this way. You see a story in the news of a woman who has lost a child suddenly. You read the story and a feeling brews up inside of you. You feel the feeling, and you send her prayers, or good wishes, for safety and security and love to get through a difficult time. I do the same for her. The only difference is that from your limited perspective, you know not that her struggle is, for all intents and purposes, unreal, as in it doesn't truly exist; it is merely an illusion based on all thoughts, words, and feelings surrounding her lives and the lives of others. As humans, you wish to end her suffering. As her equal, and a part of her, and she a part of me, I wish only to remind her of who she truly is by way of signs and messages.

L: Well, what kinds of signs and messages would God send her?

G: Flowers, chocolates, cupcakes, balloons, phone calls. Any and all manners of commune with God to let her know she is not alone. From an earthly perspective, you are all doing this as individuals. From a Godly perspective, we are all doing this for her growth and potential to wake up to the truths of the Universe. We are cocreators. We feel all feelings, always. The only difference is how we communicate those feelings by and through one another. Humans by and large miscommunicate. That is to say they do not commune with God. God always communes with them— by and through you (meaning all of you).

L: Because our souls—

G: The God within is capable of communicating messages through thoughts and feelings to one another in times of crisis and in times of joy, sadness, and elation.

L: Whoa. That is a lot to digest, but I do think I understand. I still don't think everyone reading this will be as convinced as I am, getting closer to being about the existence of God or Source Energy and our connection to it or of it, but I get it now more and more.

G: "I am closer to being." More perfect words have yet to be spoken by you and through you. When you are capable of being "I am being," then you too will be a master of the universe.

L: Thank you. I am learning, well, remembering. Now can we talk about the weather?

G: We may.

L: What gives with all this wild weather we are having, not just here but all over the world?

G: What gives indeed?

L: Why do you always respond to a question with a question?

G: Why indeed?

L: Now you are joking with me.

G: Yes. However, we will ask you again the question of why the weather has taken a dramatic turn such as it has in recent years.

L: Well, I think some would say that God is angry at us?

G: Oh, here we go again with that whole angry God notion.

L: I know that is not true, but others do believe this is part of our problem with Mother Nature. Is there a Mother Nature? Is Mother Nature a person?

G: Mother Nature is an idea, not a being. Nor is it a state of being. It is simply an idea about how your planet operates.

L: Well, then can you answer the question of why our weather can be so tempestuous and sometimes downright deadly upon our planet. Tornados, tsunamis, earthquakes, rains, floods, killer snowstorms, raging wild fires. What gives?

At the time of this writing [late September of 2017] there had been Hurricane Irma, Hurricane Maria, a massive earthquake in Mexico City as well as some smaller earthquakes in Mexico and California, and fires in Northern California. Our current president, Donald Trump, continues to shock and dismay our nation with his words and actions. The country is on pins and needles.

G: Certainly, things are seemingly bleak, but have no fear. We are here to answer each and every one of your questions. For this is all divine timing, you know.

L: It sort of does feel like that. All of this chaos is coming in the middle of the creation of the book, and oddly enough, it does feel as if it has a rhyme or reason.

G: It does, my dear. And no, you are not the cause of all this as you were thinking.

L: I was thinking that. I wrote that question, but then I erased it. Why did I erase that?

G: Fear of being judged harshly. For fear is the root cause of all suffering.

L: Which is answering my question of what the hell is going on in our world right now. Fear is at the heart of all of this? I feel as if fear is holding me back right now from writing. I have rage and fear inside of me. It feels tight and wound and as if I am bubbling over with anger, and I want to scream and rage out loud. I feel turmoil inside of me. I feel sad for our planet, sad for our world. I feel sad for our children and our children's children. What is going on here in our world, and how can we fix this?

G: You are ready now to listen and comprehend?

L: Yes. I think so.

G: Good. Then we shall begin again with this explanation. Fear is the absence of love. Only love is real and true. Only love will save your world from its current illusion. Where there is love, there is hope.

L: Do we have hope?

G: You do. It may not feel as if there is hope right now, but there is. All around you there is hope. There are people raising their hands up and saying for all to hear, "We are here for you. We will help you. We are not letting you falter." Where there is hope, there is change.

L: I do see that there is hope. It feels as if we are getting closer to saying we are not going to take this anymore. It's like a bubbling over point.

G: And what happens when you have reached the end of your proverbial rope?

L: You hold on tight and start trying to pull yourself up again. Well, at least most people would do that. Some do give up when they are at the ends of their ropes.

G: Some do, yes, but most hang on for dear life and struggle through the pain to climb back up again. That is what your world will do. It will reach the end of its rope and simply begin again. For life is a never-ending cycle of creation, and when one set of circumstances is reached, another comes to replace it.

L: All of this is well and good, but it's not answering any of my larger questions about why all of these terrible weather-related events keep happening.

G: This is the end of the rope. This is the final sprint, 1st and goal, the final chapter in this particular story. It is the be-all and end-all for the evolutionary cycle you all are currently in. Are you going to sink or swim? Fumble and falter? Score a field goal or touchdown? What happens next is fantastic, stupendous, and phenomenal. Hope springs eternal.

L: I have never understood that phrase. What does it mean?

G: Whenever you have hope, you have a new beginning. Every single time. No exception.

L: I am frustrated.

G: We feel your frustration. You are waiting for us to give you an answer that feels right, the answer the you that is "of ego" Laura wants to give. You want a clear, definable answer that tells the world this is all its fault, and you need to wake up and change so we can change our world. And we will say to you that all that is nonsense.

L: What is nonsense?

G: All of that is blame and condemnation, and we will never blame. We do not condemn, but rather, we observe. You see the world as "a mess." We see the world as perfectly imperfect with all its scars and machinations. All experiences, both good and bad, are of value in your worlds. You take the good with the bad. You do it all with grace and dignity. You do not fight against and rail about the systems of your present world. For doing that will only keep you all stuck in your present reality.

L: So then what do we do? It sounds as if you are saying we should embrace the turmoil. Does that mean we should turn a blind eye to what is happening in our present reality?

G: For that is not what we are saying at all. What we are saying is to not place attention where the illusions occur. Do not suffer fools. We would simply say to feel your feelings about the current illusions, but do not dwell upon them. See them for what they are.

L: So look at them, but understand that they are just that, illusions? But that still seems as if you are telling us to turn a blind eye and not help the people who are suffering at the hands of these hurricanes, earthquakes, or fires. People have lost their homes, their livelihoods. Children have lost their lives. No way can you just tell us to turn a blind eye. You here have also said that in order to receive, we must give. So shouldn't we be donating money and food and supplies? Shouldn't we be offering them hope, which you say is so all important?

G: For you have answered your own question here. We do not say to turn a blind eye. We do not say ignore what is happening and walk away. We simply say do not dwell upon the illusion. Simply see the illusion for what it is. Then once you have looked upon the situation, from a space of knowing and oneness with the Universe, only then may you be of service to them. To give from this vantage point is to say, "I see your illusion, and I offer up my hope and faith that a new day will spring upon you that brings joy and happiness and a promise of a better life. As you rebuild, may you begin again, and in that new beginning you shall be healed."

L: So if I ask again why all of these terrible things are happening in our world, am I dwelling on the illusion?

G: You are, but we will indulge you and further the conversation if you wish.

L: I wish.

G: So ask away. What is your question? We will answer always.

L: Why on earth did three hurricanes occur back-to-back causing so much destruction?

G: You were going to say death and destruction, but you decided not to. Why do you think that is?

L: Because while there were deaths, it was not a catastrophic amount of deaths.

G: Do you think that is by design?

L: I guess.

G: No. You know. Yet you fear saying it here because you do not wish to upset the fallen and their loved ones.

L: True.

G: In every illusion, there is a grandiose experiment.

L: And what is that?

G: Can you find the hope? Is there a miracle in the mess?

L: I think I understand what you are saying here, in that even with all of the destruction, there are moments where we could be grateful that more people were not killed or that even though homes were destroyed, most lives were saved.

G: Is the message here not the same as what happened in your 9/11 massacre? Has hope sprung eternal again and again?

L: I understand. I do not like it, but I understand. Was it a coincidence that these storms all happened around the time of 9/11?

G: There are no coincidences. Of this we have told you. Of this you know and have faith.

L: So yet again we are being tested?

G: You are not being tested. This is not a math quiz, no. You are merely at the effect of your cause. This is the explanation you have been waiting for, and here it is. Though we do not need to further explain it again, we will, for the sake of all who have yet to comprehend fully the notion that you are all (at form level) responsible for the all of everything that happens upon your world. You are all of one mind, thinking and creating through the power of your thoughts the experiences within and upon your world. Each and every one of the all is at cause. One does not and cannot think alone. All minds are creating experiences together. Therefore, whenever such circumstances arise where fear is so frontal lobe, so top of mind, an experience will thus then be created for the all of humanity, which manifests the fear mindset.

What you are experiencing is the All of Everything bringing unto itself that which is most feared—death, destruction, betrayal, and abandonment.

L: Wow. I mean just wow. I know it, but I guess I still can't believe it. So then is it safe to say this is all Donald Trump's fault?

G: You laugh, but there is truth in jesting. The circumstances of fear's manifestations arising are in fact related to the events in your nation occurring currently. Though we do not deem him "at fault," as you say, we would agree that the actions of one have affected the whole. We have told you prior he is a teacher, a shower of truth, and a shiner of light on that which must be healed in your nation.

L: So then all of these weather-related incidents have nothing to do with climate change?

G: No.

L: Seriously? You know that is what most people would believe. It's what I thought was the cause.

G: You, and they, would be misinformed in your thinking that this is the sole cause of these storms.

L: Is it at all related? Not even a little bit?

G: No.

L: But you just said it is not the "sole cause," which would imply it was partially to blame?

G: A misinterpretation.

L: Dear God, may you please accurately interpret this for me.

G: We shall hereby say "soul" cause. This is not the *soul* cause of these tragedies. Here we applaud you for this instantaneous prayer. In your asking we clarified. Your progress is remarkable on this front. We are humbled and proud.

L: You told me in spirit form we have no need for those emotions.

G: We are speaking in human words right now. So humble and proud would apply here.

L: Well, thank you. And your clarification now makes perfect sense. Sole and soul. Climate change is not the "soul" cause. You have said that we are destroying our planet, though, piece by piece, little by little.

G: We have said that you are treating this planet unkindly, yes, and taking for granted all of its natural resources. This is a fact. This is not however, a related cause to the current weather atrocities.

L: So how is Trump responsible for this?

G: He does not shoulder full responsibility, in that all minds are joined. His individual consciousness, however, is of such a magnitude of anger and resentment toward his fellow man that he has created within each individual and the collective consciousness an epidemic of fear and irrational thought. It is from this space of fear that all manifestations of a weather relatedness have stemmed.

L: Why? Why would that happen? How can we all be doing this?

G: It is simple law of attraction. That which is like unto itself is drawn. Dwell in and upon fear, fear is made manifest in your reality as "acts of God," as your theologians would have you believe. In actuality, universal law predicates (pre-dictates) all that happens in and of your external world vision.

L: Well, then where do we go from here? How do we heal, and most importantly, how do we stop all of this chaos?

G: As we have said, stop thinking about it as you have deemed it, chaos. Start seeing it for what it is: an illusion of separation from your source. Then may we discuss what is next.

L: Fine. How, then, may we heal from this illusion and move to a better place?

G: Move to a better place internally. Within each citizen is placed an inner guidance system, which knows the truth. Go within or you will go without. We have said this to many masters in many different ways. Go to the place within that knows the truth of who and what you really are. Find that place, and stay there for as long as you can, as much as you can. Bless that space, that place within, as your sacred, eternal beingness. Be there now.

L: And if we don't?

G: Then will you be stuck within the illusion. In any given moment, should one return to the Creator and all its creations and declare they are one with the All That Is, will a metaphysical hand be outstretched to lift them out of the illusion-based world they are living in.

L: What about praying for them? If we send prayers, will they resonate through them? You say all minds are joined. So would they hear my prayers in a sense?

G: It all depends upon the prayer. A prayer of supplication and surrender is rightly justified, as it reminds them of where they came from. A prayer of strategy and sanctity would merely keep them stuck within their illusion.

L: You lost me there. Can you please speak in more simple terms?

G: As always, we are glad you asked for clarification. Supplication and surrender—"I am one with God and the All That Is. Together may we bind all minds and hearts so that we may see this situation for what it is, an illusion brought about by a fear-based thought system. Together we shall turn from the illusion and declare that only love is real."

L: And the other prayer you mentioned, strategy and sanctity?

G: "Dear God, please lead me out of this mess I am in."

L: So that won't work?

G: Not for one who believes in a God who will rescue only the righteous few. For some who understand the oneness from which we all are a part and apart of, it may very well suffice. For most, it would not, which is why we share it here with you. Prayer only works when it comes coupled with belief. We cannot stress this point enough. You would do well to shout this from the rooftops wherever you may go to share this work.

L: And how do we get to that belief because the fact is that finding that inner belief is difficult, especially when you see the chaos (er, illusion) surrounding us.

G: See the magic within that chaos (your word, not ours). See it as the miracle that it is trying to be. Tell it, "Thank you, for showing me the light and the way out of misery." Declare, "For this is not real," and "I am."

L: I am what?

G: I am truth. I am the Universe. I am one with the All That Is. I am the All of Everything. I am.

L: Today I had a notion while at the gym.

G: Inspired thought.

L: All right, inspired thought. My thought was that everything that we desire in earnest in our own life already exists as possibility, which is why we desire it so heavily in the first place.

G: Give us an example.

L: For me it would be having more kids or wanting to be a speaker and sharing my story and this material with others. I desire these things because they exist as possibility in my experience. Therefore, if I were capable of full-out belief that they already exist for me, I would be able to draw them into my experience. The only stopping point for their manifestation would be the presence of fear in my life about them.

G: A miraculously accurate presentation of spiritual laws and principles. As we have inscribed here previously, though you had yet to understand it fully, everything you have ever been and ever will be exists as possibility because in some universal plane it has already happened. The only way to know something is to experience this within your present reality. Therefore, you draw to you any experiences which you have presently thought about in any and all lifetimes. You cannot not be that which you are wanting to be (in the absence of fear), because you have already been this before in other planes of existence and experience. Therefore, whatever it is you are desiring to be, we would tell you to be it in your mind and in your actions and reactions. Be that which you already are, because you already are.

L: Oddly enough that makes perfect sense to me.

G: To you who are remembering at a rapid pace, it will feel like truth. For those seeking enlightenment it would need further explanation.

L: I finally started telling people about this book and with whom I am writing it.

G: As we knew you would.

L: It is scary.

G: We know.

L: It terrifies me to put myself out there in this way. And yet it feels as if this is what I am meant to be doing. Yet I see so many other people sharing similar books, and I get scared (yet again) that I won't be able to make this my new career or new reality. I am back to the mediocre feeling I get about who I am. I am back to feeling unworthy. The same cyclical patterns return again.

G: Forever we shall heal this notion of unworthiness in you. Declare here and now, "I am worthy. I am a teacher of spiritual principle. I am truth. I am love. I am."

L: I am worthy. I am a teacher of spiritual principle. I am truth. I am love. I am.

G: Now say this every day until you live it, until you believe it as truth, which it is. You are capable of healing the world. You all are. There is no one more special than the next. For each of you is a teacher, a healer, a mentor. Some of you are just better at it than others. So it is upon those of us who are clear, concise communicators to communicate to the masses that which is right about how our worlds work both internally and externally. You are all of God. Good dwells within. God dwells within. The Oneness, Universal Presence, Source of all being. It matters not what you call the "I Am," which you are all born from; it matters only that you embrace the ideas and principles. You must live it so that you may be it.

L: It?

G: Be at peace. Be at harmony. Be at—

I hear and feel nothing. I sit quietly and hear nothing and actually feel at peace for a minute.

G: One with the Universe. When you are at one with the Universe, you are at peace, which is how you have been made to feel.

L: It feels good. Oh my god. It feels so good to be at peace. I want that feeling always.

G: And you may have it always. Whenever you are ready, we are ready to guide you back to love. Amen.

L: How will I know when it's time to stop writing, when this book is done?

G: This book will never be done from a spiritual standpoint. You will continue to create and question, and we will continue to answer and inspire. As for this particular material, which we would call "The All of Everything," we will tell you when it is time to stop and share. You are getting close; of this we know you are sure.

9 God—The Interview, Part Four

"Dear God, please remove from these pages any and all words and material that do not serve the highest good of my being and the highest good of all who come to read this. May we remember together the truths of the universe. Amen."

Laura: Who is Dr. Peebles?

God: He was a teacher for you, your first real teacher of a metaphysical nature.

L: Is that why I heard the name Peebles that day in my massage?

G: You have heard many messages of a psychic nature, which you have largely ignored. Your intuitiveness made it possible to hear and remember.

L: Remember what?

G: Who this man is in relation to you.

L: And who is he in relation to me?

G: He is you, he is me. He is all of us. Therefore, he communicates to those seeking spiritual enlightenment of a different kind. One who seeks to know God completely and fully, without any preconceived notions of who and what the universe actually is from the concept outside of the earthy plane, may speak to and with Dr. Peebles.

L: And why would you need to have no preconceived notions?

G: Fear keeps you stuck in beliefs that do not serve the soul's higher purpose, which is to experience itself fully in all planes of existence. If you were to see yourself as solely a human being, well, then you are not being truthful with your soul self.

L: So only those who have a knowing that we are more than just human beings would be able to communicate with this Peebles guy?

G: It is not necessary to believe fully in this concept. However, if and when one's curiosity is piqued, then that person shall seek and find the answers within.

L: So, in a sense, he is within all of us?

G: In so much that we are all one, yes.

L: So this is how a multitude of people are able to channel him?

G: Precisely. And those whose curiosity has been piqued heretofore will go and find Peebles's teachings for themselves.

L: Well, they will certainly find something uniquely interesting. It's almost comical.

G: You are laughing, yet you also enjoyed his teachings.

L: I did. I found them funny, and yet some of them resonated with me. The more we write here, the more I start to believe it. All of it. I have to say I am crazy proud of this book. I am consistently fascinated that I was able to write it.

G: This is because we wrote it together. You, me, and we. Together.

L: I think I am finally getting all of this. Today, I reached out to a friend in the hopes of gaining some advice on getting it published. Immediately he launched into the whys of how hard it is to get a book deal and the difficulties of marketing the book. In the past, I would have jumped right into fear and the knowing that he was right. I may have agreed with him and given up. However, in my knowing did I stay true that these words are meant to be shared whether it's two people or twenty million people. So I will move forward in knowing and not fear. How best can I help myself to make sure these works are published and shared?

G: You know this answer. You have no need to ask us anymore.

L: I do. Give it to God. Here I shall say, "Dear God, as we have cocreated this material together, so shall we share it together with the masses. Let fear be wiped away as we share these truths, our truths, with all who come seeking it. Bring forth the perfect people, places, and circumstances to get this book published and to the masses of minds waiting for answers. Amen."

G: Perfection. Absolute perfection. So shall it be done. So shall we share this book with the masses. Amen.

L: And then it is upon me to not denigrate into fear via the ego or doubt and worry?

G: As you speak, so shall you be. As you share, so shall this be shared. Care not who reads it. Care only who has written it. Know that Laura is worthy of its sharing, and only then may it be received by the many.

L: I have been rereading this material over and over. In moments of weakness and irrational thoughts and fear, I return to this book, which I, which we, have written. It makes me weep with shock and joy and sadness and elation. I have typed all of these words and answered these questions simply by listening to the quiet inner voice inside my head. And the words are incredible, insightful, and amazing. Yet half of what we have written here I don't even remember writing. How do I know these things? How could I have written all of this so easily, so effortlessly, and with such intensity? I stand here and tell you that Laura Saltman, the creator of this book, has not the knowledge or drive to have created this book on her own. Yet, even as I say this, I can honestly admit my fears, doubts,

and worries still prevail. I can read all of this and believe in the concepts, yet I still lack—

G: Faith.

L: I still lack faith. Sometimes. Not always. I can preach and teach this to anyone who calls me or texts me or comes seeking advice, but when it comes to me, man, I get caught up in my doubt.

G: It is not only faith that you are lacking here. Perseverance and persistence are you current enemies as well.

L: Persistence meaning consistency of practice?

G: Consistency of practice, but also the persistence to move through the chain.

L: The chain?

G: The chain of command, which guards the mind.

L: I don't follow.

G: Of course you don't. This is why we are here to explain and unravel the mysteries of our universe.

L: What chain of command?

G: Who is actually in charge in most, if not all, thinking?

L: The ego.

G: So where does lack of persistence start?

L: With the ego?

G: Precisely. Ego thinks first.

L: But you earlier said that "first thought" is always the right thought. So that is a contradiction, isn't it?

G: "Consistency of practice" is what we are unraveling right now.

L: As in unraveling the mystery of it?

G: Yes. "First thought" is always the right thought when it comes to any rational thought. I am perfect. I am beautiful. I am a good dancer. I am a healer. I am going to make a peanut butter and jelly sandwich right now because I am hungry. I want tuna fish even though I should probably stick to fruit. Which of these seems like an irrational thought?

L: Wanting something but then putting the "but I should probably do this" scenario into it?

G: Very good. Irrational thought is of the ego. I want. I need. I must have. I don't want it. I don't like it. I can't do it. I can't have it. I don't want to do it right now. No way am I capable of doing this. This house is never going to sell. This job is terrible. Nobody likes me. No one will hire me.

L: Whenever it comes from fear, that is how we indicate to ourselves this is an ego thought?

G: The chain of command starts with the ego. I am *not* good enough. I am *not* worthy. Whoever goes seeking spiritual enlightenment and to know God and to be one with the Universal Presence is at war with the ego. Ego commands the army. Ego has tried many times to write this book. Rational thought (Holy Spirit) shares truth and love. Soul knows all.

L: So then what is the chain of command?

G: Ego thought. God thought. Soul thought.

L: That does not seem right.

G: And why not?

L: Because if I were writing this, I would have said ego thought. Holy Spirit thought. Soul thought.

G: Shall we ask for the proper answer?

L: Yes.

G: "Dear Universal Presence, please share with us the truth in this matter at hand. Amen." You may ask your question again.

L: So then what is the chain of command?

G: God thought is all thought.

L: So there is no chain of command? There is no ego?

G: Ego is illusion thought, all thoughts that are not of God. I am *not* worthy. I am unhappy, scared, sad.

L: So there is ego, which is essentially any thought where we are not thinking like God and from love.

G: Exactly. Any thought that comes from love is of God. Any fear-based thought comes from ego. Ego is not in charge.

L: So stop letting ego run the show.

G: Stop letting ego do anything.

L: We were discussing consistency of practice, and you—

G: We.

L: We said that ego thinks first, but now you are saying all thought is God thought. So I don't think I understand.

G: So we shall explain in further detail. Ego thought is all ungodly, irrational thought. It comes up naturally in defense of spiritual truth. For this is how all illusions come to take shape and form. Whenever one seeks to know oneself as the Oneness (or God as most call it), our ego swoops in to say, "Hey, don't forget about me. I'm here to ruin your day and your plans. There is no God, you silly creature. What kind of God would rain down plagues upon our citizens? You can't afford that house, buy that car, or get that job. You are not good enough." General Ego has commanded his troops to attack your psyche, and it shoots to kill. "Command not the God within, you shall follow my orders and do as I say!" This is how Hitler came into power with no mere mortal really questioning him at first. Pure ego running the show.

L: Oh boy, we are back to Hitler again here.

G: Who better than to teach this powerful lesson. I told you earlier he was a teacher to you, to all of you. Hitler commanded his troops by the sheer force of his ego. His will to inflict harm was laser focused. Not one being upon earth dared reason with him for fear (his own ego thought) of death sentenced upon him. Better for others to suffer than them, the ego reasoned.

L: Where are you going with all of this?

G: Suffice it to say the inner battle is waged whenever one's ego (irrational mind) is the general in charge. The way out of the ego's clutches is to turn back to the one who created all of everything—to think with the mind of God. I am capable. I am able to be persistent in my practice because my soul is in charge. My soul knows what is best for me. We conquer our ego whenever we think as one mind. We are one, we are.

L: As in "I am that I am."

G: Simple. Isn't it?

L: Well, based on that explanation, I would not call all of this simple. I would call it quite complicated.

G: Not when you persistently remind oneself. Re-mind yourself of the truth.

L: I think I know where I got lost now. I went back and reread this whole section on consistency of practice, and when you said "ego thinks first," you were referring to that one point. Whenever you are undertaking consistency of practice, ego thinks first. My interpretation initially was wrong, which is why I felt it was a contradiction of an earlier point made about first thought.

G: How one interprets is paramount in the remembering process of evolution. Here will we say all spiritual beings seeking spiritual truths must know clarification is necessary and always available, and one should always seek answers within first. This is not to say the information may not be accurate. Merely are we reminding all who seek enlightenment to go within in times of confusion or in times when clarity is needed.

L: So then I need to go back and ask the question about your statement "all thought is God thought," and so I shall say, "Dear God, please help to explain the seeming contradiction between all thought and ego thought."

G: All—the All of Everything, which is you and me and we, together we are one mind, and therefore, every thought comes from the All. As bodies, we become body-mind-spirit individually and collectively. In this dichotomy is where the ego comes into play. All thought does emanate from God or the Oneness. This is incontrovertible fact. All thoughts are creative. This is also incontrovertible fact. All minds think alike. Not a fact. As bodies, the All of Everything are capable of seeing and thinking of themselves as separated from the All of Everything.

Thoughts that emanated from the All are then split apart from the Everything into the nothing where they become susceptible to irrationality. To re-mind themselves of the true nature of their being returns them to Source Energy. Thoughts rebind back to the all.

L: My head is spinning. This is tough to understand, yet I think I also do understand. I would imagine there will be those who read this book and will be completely lost.

G: Not necessarily but yes, these concepts are cyclical in nature in that we return back to the same principles over and over with different explanations and connotations. Consistency of practice aids in the re-minding process.

L: Why do you say it as re-mind instead of remind?

G: To remind oneself of one's true nature, that is re-mind back with the Oneness, the All of Everything.

L: So I would imagine when reading this book that it may help to reread it many times until we are reminded of these spiritual truths.

G: Precisely, as well may all who undertake its reading be reminded to ask for help and guidance using the voice within for any necessary clarification during the reading, watching, or listening process.

L: I still have so many questions I wish to ask. I could go on for 500 books. Some questions are silly and some serious. I have to know the answer to this one. Working in

entertainment news, it always seems that celebrities die in threes. It's a phenomenon that has been proven time and time again? What gives?

G: Need we remind you of the cyclical nature of all of everything? Need we again repeat the body-mind-spirit trifecta? Tri (three) is the natural cycle of evolution. Therefore, it repeats itself in all of life, in all of existence. Mom, dad, child. Ego, conscious, super conscious. We three kings leave the earth as one.

Today is October 2, 2017. Our world has been rocked again by yet another mass shooting. This time, in Las Vegas, where a man opened fire from his hotel window and killed fifty-nine people, injuring over 500 others.

L: Dear God, as we open our lines of communication here again may we bind all minds together to reveal our truth. Amen. If you are here with me, let me know.

G: We are here. We told you earlier we would convene this evening did we not?

L: You did.

G: We have many answers for you. So let us begin. But first let us pray again. "Dear God, as we move through these difficult times together, may we explain universal truths so that all who come to this material may be healed by its magnificence. Amen."

L: You just prayed to yourself?

G: Not to myself, through all of us. Together may we release the notion that prayer be undertaken only by the ones in body form.

L: So spirits also pray? God prays?

G: Of course God prays. Prayer is a universal concept in which all minds conjoin in chorus. As you pray, so shall I too. I see your tears. I see your triumphs. I pray with you and for you.

L: God prays for us?

G: What do you think we do all day?

L: Well, I certainly don't think you sit around praying for our world. We need some major prayers today; that is for sure. How does this happen to somebody? What goes wrong in the mind?

G: How can we explain the actions of another without first looking at the actions of the whole?

L: So yet again you are going to say that this act of violence was brought about by the collective consciousness?

G: Fellow man manifests that which unto itself is drawn whenever a choir of voices gathers. Where better to administer chaos than a venue of music and celebration. In all of these mass shootings, a pattern is developing for all the world to see. I shall strike down your way of life through disruption and destruction. Here may my guns create a sense of panic and unrest among world leaders.

L: What is the pattern?

G: We know you know the answer. However, we will indulge you with our explanation. The pattern is that which among your world leaders has yet to be addressed. No man shall take another man's life unless and until he has shared bread with another.

L: What the heck does that even mean?

G: Where do all men gather upon the battlefield?

L: The front lines?

G: No silly, the mess hall. All men gather to break bread in times of war. It is only in times of war and the necessary breaking down of criminal acts carried out upon one another that one has any need ever for guns. Remove them from a sullied hand, and here you shall begin to undo this pattern of men.

L: Women have carried out gun attacks though in the past.

G: Attacks upon men and upon those who have damaged their pride perhaps, but in your current world, no. Women are mostly incapable of these types of heinous acts in part for their fear of retribution and detainment.

L: Sometimes I wonder while I am writing, "Can this really be the truth?" But yet I also think, "Why on earth would I ever write that?" because I honestly would never think that way.

G: That is why it is upon you to share this information as such.

L: This does not address the underlying issue at hand of how to stop these mass shootings in America.

G: It does address the underlying issue in that guns are unnecessary for anyone but your military personnel and crime fighters.

L: But that is not happening.

G: We feel your frustration building in that you want a different answer, and yet the answer will always remain the same.

L: I know, but aren't we creating these attacks through our mass consciousness of fear?

G: Focused attention upon any issue brings to light any and all scenarios from which to grow and evolve. This issue is of utter importance in your world, and yet continually does the issue arise. Repeated scenarios occur for transformation, and yet no one among your leaders of the nation dares raise the issue for fear of reconstitution.

L: Why do I feel like you mean rewriting the constitution?

G: Because we do, and we know you know this too. As it stands, the current constitution is no longer an accurate representation of the world you are currently living in. The right to bear arms no longer works in a world where obtaining a gun license is easier than obtaining a driver's license. Yet not one among your current administration or one who has come before dares touch the sacred political bible for fear of being ousted from his or her current position of power and influence. The mere thought of undertaking such a painful, arduous battle strikes fear in the heart of anyone willing to entertain the notion. Yet this is what is needed for conditions of your world to change.

L: I know it and many, many Americans know it. It has been said many times by lots of people. Yet you are right. I would imagine that no one in Washington is willing to risk such a radical endeavor.

G: Radical makes change. Repetition makes chaos.

L: I fear we may never move past this issue. If a gunman murdering school children does not cause a change, then certainly this incident won't stop the violence.

G: Then that is what you will see in your current world view. For this is the problem of all soldiers in the fight for spiritual enlightenment: the idea that something cannot ever change. For this is simply not true. Should a radical shift occur, undertaken by all who wish to see a different world, then that is what you will see. A few can affect millions. As difficult as this notion is to undertake, it is very much your truth, all of your truths.

L: So how can I do this? How can my one little thought and prayer change the minds of millions?

G: My dear Laura. What have we been teaching you here, or rather, shall we say, reminding you? What is possible when all minds join when you know we are all of one mind?

L: We may affect the whole?

G: Yes, the All of Everything hears your cries for help. Your acceptance of spiritual truth binds it to all others. For no one person can change the world, but one person can change their own world.

L: I have heard this before, but what does it actually mean?

G: In order to change the outer world, you must first change your inner world. As you think, so shall you be. As you grow and evolve, so shall you believe. As you believe, so shall you unmask a spiritual awakening upon all others whose minds are bound along with the All of Everything.

L: So I really can help make a difference in our world by a simple prayer for it?

G: Not a simple prayer, an unveiling of the radical idea of oneness for all to hear. May we join minds, not hands, in prayer.

L: And what would that prayer be?

G: "Dear God, as we look upon our world, which seemingly is falling apart, may we know the truth of our oneness. In our holiness of spiritual truth may we be healed. Accepting this truth for myself, I share it with my beloved brethren. Together may we endure through tragedy and triumph as a nation touched by our souls, capable of creating a new constitution where all may be treated as equal under the law. Amen."

L: Why am I still so fearful about the releasing of this book? Will it be successful? Will people buy it? Will anyone want to read it? I have seen other books by authors who claim to "talk

to God," and other than Neale Donald Walsch's book, they all seem to go pretty much unnoticed in the mainstream.

G: And why do you think that is?

L: I don't know. That is why I am asking you.

G: Change the channel.

L: What does that mean?

G: You are the channel guide. You decide which programs to share. If you don't like the channel, change it.

L: I still don't understand.

G: Make manifest your version of reality. What is it that you choose and accept for this material?

L: I choose and accept for this book to reach the masses and to be on the best-seller list. I choose and accept to make my living being a speaker and teacher of spiritual truth to those willing to listen and those seeking a better way of life.

G: Then so it shall be done for and unto you.

L: So why did other channels write books or other material and they barely made a dent? What makes someone an Eckhart Tolle and another a kooky lady surrounded by her candles? This is a not a judgement, merely an observation and a question.

G: Thank you for clarifying. What makes someone fit to teach this material is being one who speaks and sees the truth all at once. You speak spiritual principles all the time to others, and while you may get caught up in daily dramas, you see our miracles every day. For in the clouds today did you not ask for a miracle and promptly did we not show you one?

L: Yes. You did. Heart in the sky. You sent me a heart-shaped cloud, which I had asked you to do moments before I saw it.

G: Your focused intention to know and receive these messages is what binds them to you.

L: So how do I know I won't share this book and it will go largely unnoticed as so many of my other projects have in the past? I just heard you say passion?

G: Passion pleads for progress. Put passion in the mix, and you have the potion for the most magical elixir in all of the universe—purpose. Peace is your purpose, we have told you earlier right here in this material. Whenever you are at purpose you are at peace.

L: I am at peace when I am writing this. I enjoy this. I enjoy enlightening people and waking them up. I love to help people. I want to help people. I desire to help people. I want to stand on stages and wake people up and shake their belief systems to their cores. I want to show them that they too can see the signs and messages for themselves.

G: Then you can, and you will. If you believe, you can achieve.

L: I need help with that, though, because my fear really knocks me down. My past history—

G: Excuse me, but we must interrupt here. Your history, in this current lifetime, will show that you created precisely the job you wanted since childhood.

L: True.

G: While others who do what you do only dreamed of working on TV the way you did.

L: True. I did create that, didn't I?

G: Yet here we are again, and you have any doubt you are capable of being that which you say you want to be?

L: You are right. It's my fear of unworthiness.

G: In the past. It is keeping you stuck in past habitual patterns of thought, which no longer serve you. You are a worthy soldier in this spiritual game.

L: And how do I shake the unworthiness off of me.

G: "Dear God, (we have said this similarly before) together we shall share this material, as cocreators, with the masses as we seek to enlighten those who wish to remember who and what they really are—perfect children of the Universe capable of creating in the image and likeness of the Oneness. Amen."

L: I am worthy. I am capable of cocreation. I am at peace.

G: Very good, my child. Very good.

L: Just when I feel I am ready to wrap this book up, so many new questions arise for me. Were all of the things that happened during the course of the writing of this book all part of the process for me, from a spiritual standpoint?

G: Yes. All points made were from a particular reference point. Your vantage point is purposeful for this material. As we go further with other books and material, you will find this purposeful creation meaningful from the standpoint of the inscriber.

L: But I am a cocreator. Doesn't that yet again negate me controlling my experience?

G: We are cocreators. That which is like unto itself is drawn. All experiences are of value, be they good or bad. There is no one experience about which you are inscribing that was necessarily "meant to be," nor shall we say it was not meant to be. All minds create together, and as we have said, all possibilities exist simultaneously. Therefore, we have a multitude of experiences from which to inscribe. There are plenty of circumstances based on your thoughts, words, and actions we may write about here with you and for you.

L: Are things "meant to be"? Do things "happen for a reason" as the cliché says?

G: Nothing "happens for a reason," as you say, other than you being the reason for its happening.

L: So then we are not meant to meet a specific person, like

a soulmate or a best friend? We are not meant to move to a specific house or take a specific trip? I ask because it has felt this way to me in the past. I was robbed one time and though it was a terrifying experience, I ended up taking a trip of a lifetime because of it. The home I currently live in, I feel as if I was guided here, and it was kismet that the home owners knew my friends in Los Angeles.

G: Not one thing happens without there having been a thought about it prior. Let us look at the examples you have given. The man who stole your purse, for example. He knocked you down and ran off. Had you not worried repeatedly while pulling into your garage about having to walk to the front door alone at night?

L: Yes. Oh my goodness, I did. I forgot about that. I had at night, but it was broad daylight when this happened.

G: Would you rather it had been at night?

L: Well, of course not.

G: So you drew to yourself an experience from which to grow and evolve, and yet you were unharmed and unscathed financially. You also, at the time, had been thinking about taking a vacation, and yet you had never done anything about said notion, true?

L: True. So because of my fear about the walk from my garage to the door, I created an experience for myself of being robbed. And because I had wanted to take a vacation, I created the perfect circumstances for that experience as well?

G: A somewhat accurate presentation, yes. Now let us take the example of your love life. After your son's father left, did you not write a note to God asking for help to please send you someone to love, pleading for a change in your circumstances?

L: I honestly don't remember doing that, but perhaps I did. I think I remember saying something like that, but I don't recall writing it down. I do recall making a list of qualities I wanted to find in a partner.

G: The answer is yes, you did write it down after a friend with psychic ability told you to do this using *The Secret*, which had been written and produced many years earlier.

L: Perhaps.

G: You drew into your experience a man suffering from similar life experiences to create a relationship with based on your thoughts, words, and action. Think the thoughts. Put the words on paper. Take action. Look for dates online or other places.

L: I see your point. What about finding my current home? I did set a lot of intentions and say a lot of prayers to find the perfect house in the perfect neighborhood. So to me it feels as if it was meant to be, as if I was guided here in my asking. My friends I have made feel as if I have known them forever and as if we were all meant to meet. I love them dearly.

G: And they you. That which is like unto itself is drawn. We will make this point again here, and we shall say you all cocreated an experience together from which to grow and evolve. For each of you had your own reasoning for reconciling.

L: Reconciling?

G: Reconvening.

L: Meaning we had been together in other lifetimes?

G: Congregations are made whenever souls desire and thoughts align. Here we shall say you return to the familiar over and over and over again, through many lifetimes in many, many forms.

L: So is this why people say it feels as if it's meant to be? Simply because we have already been together in other lifetimes? I have thought this to be the case. Are you saying I am correct?

G: You are correct. It feels as if something is meant to be because you have already been it.

L: Well, that's a first, because most of what we have written here is a direct contradiction of how I thought this whole Universe thing worked. Well, can you answer me this? The people who died in Las Vegas who all congregated at a concert, were they meant to all be together on that day for that horrible tragedy?

G: Limited minds in one evening cannot grasp yet the magnitude of your beingness. Mere mortals are you who do not yet understand the purpose and meaning of each lifetime. Circumstances dictated scenarios that led to the massacre at the hands of a gunman who I told you earlier (though you used your free will to erase it) acted un-alone in his hotel room.

L: Was another person with him in the room or are you speaking metaphysically?

G: We are speaking metaphysically, of course.

L: Why do you say it as un-alone?

G: The word does not matter. The meaning is the same. Circumstances surrounding his life demanded action. The action he took is in direct correlation with all thoughts, words, and deeds of all who came to congregate that evening.

L: Oh my god. So you are saying that they all created themselves being murdered? I just don't get that. I'm sorry, but I can't comprehend for the life of me how someone is responsible for his or her death at the hands of a madman.

G: A madman. A madwoman. A bus. A fallen tree. A rope tied around one's own neck. Responsibility lies with the ones who created the experience for themselves to grow and evolve their souls.

L: So our soul is running the show, then? Does that mean that our bodies and minds have no control in anything?

G: For this is not what we are saying at all. We are simply saying one cannot befall if one has not bespoken.

L: Your words don't make any sense to me. May you please speak in more simplistic terms here?

G: We shall say to all who are ready to listen that nothing happens to you that is not through you. Thoughts. Words. Actions. The binding mechanism of repeated thoughts placed within one's mind and body bare the fruit and are made manifest as one's ultimate reality. Nary shall you be one who seeks ancient wisdom without knowing this binary truth. Thoughts are binding whether you believe them or not.

L: So if you believe you may get shot at a concert, what, you are screwed? I seriously doubt anyone went to that concert thinking—

G: About all those poor souls in Manchester or Orlando? Those school children in Connecticut? The people on the train, the bus, the movie theater? Subconscious thoughts are the demons of the mind. They stay hidden, eating away at you from inside. Conscious beliefs are the roots of our souls. They need to be watered and fed and tended to consistently.

L: So no one consciously went to the concert thinking these horrible things could happen? It had been implanted in their subconscious minds? How, then, can we change these subconscious thoughts especially if we don't know about them? That's dangerous and scary.

G: And you have hit the nail on the head yet again here. Subconscious thoughts are the most powerful tool in ego's arsenal. It preys upon them, it nurses those wounds repeatedly. To change subconscious thoughts, one must undertake conscious prayer and intention to release them by asking oneself, "What fears am I holding onto today? And here I shall release them now to the nothing from which they have come to me. These thoughts serve no one but the ego, and here I shall release them to God and all of the Universe. Amen."

L: Yet again you offer a simple solution, and here again I must ask, is it really that simple?

G: And here we shall say (repeated again) it is that simple whenever one undertakes consistent, daily practice. Exercise, eat right, and get right spiritually each and every day, and my goodness, what a magnificent life you would all lead. Yet who among you, save for your spiritual leaders, has undertaken such practical advice?

L: Not many.

G: Not many indeed. Consistency of practice is paramount in evolvement of the soul.

L: Why can't the soul stop these tragic events? If the soul knows what's best for us, why can't it put a stop to it? Why didn't my dad's soul stop him from taking his own life?

G: We have said here before one's own life is just that, one's own. You may do with it as you like, for this is your free will. Soul knows best just as *Father Knows Best* (we liked that show very much), Father being the All of Everything. For a soul to intervene would be to violate one's free will, and we will never do that. It defies the laws of the universe. Soul may mock you, rock you, shock you, and use other mechanisms with which to wake you up, but the soul may never violate your free will. If it is your wish to leave an earthly plane (or any other plane) and your soul has tried all ways to wake you, there is nothing more to be done in the matter.

L: Well, that explains suicide, but what about the concert goers? Couldn't the soul stop what was happening to them?

G: Soul seeks to grow and evolve, and in its perspective, death is not a punishment but a release. Therefore, a soul cannot and will not intervene in any said circumstance.

L: This makes me sad as a human being though, because I am looking at the faces of the fifty-nine people killed in the Las Vegas shooting, and I am angry and sad and can't comprehend how there is a reason for that. How do I explain when someone asks me, "How can a God let these things happen? Clearly this is pure evil." How can I explain to those grieving their loved ones, whose lives were cut short tragically, all of this without sounding trite? Because to me, if someone were speaking to me in this manner after a terrible tragedy like this, I would probably want to punch that person in the face.

G: From where you are standing now, it is only your job to comfort the grieving not to explain the truth.

L: So what would I say in a time like this?

G: "To all who are grieving, I feel your pain; I share your darkness. A life not lived fully is tragic. My heart aches for your suffering."

L: So don't try to bring up any spiritual notions whatsoever. Don't try to inspire and uplift?

G: One cannot uplift from a place of spiritual knowing those who are grieving. When they are ready, though, they will come to you. Seek thee who shall re-mind us back to love so that we may remember who we truly all are. Upon one's "death" all truths shall be revealed. Until then, those in body form are guided to our teachers whenever they are ready to learn. From this place of darkness they shall seek the light.

L: What if someone who is reading this book doesn't believe in any of it? What if they get to the end and think this is all made-up trash?

G: Then so be it. It is not upon anyone to judge another's path to salvation. For in the end, all will know the truth. For it is up to them whether they learn it in this lifetime or another.

L: Why can't I stay in that high place and live this truth? Why is this so hard? I continue in these ups and downs and highs and lows. One day I am whistling a happy tune, and the next I am in panic mode about where my next dollar is coming from. I thank you, and then I question you. Why is that?

G: For this is an excellent way to explain the truth of the human experience. It's peaks and valleys. It's ups and downs. It's hard work being human. It's easy being a soul. Soul seeks to know and experience through you. Yet you are human. So stop beating yourself up on days where being a spiritual being isn't easy. It's difficult work all of this, for all of you. Even spiritual leaders in human form get tripped up, have bad moments. Perhaps not bad days, as it were, but bad moments for sure.

L: Why only bad moments?

G: Because they know how to pull themselves up out of the dark. Right quick action, intentional prayer, focusing one's breath. These are all tools to stem the tide.

L: I try that. I really do. It is just so hard to lose the fear when you are in a place where you feel lost.

G: For once I was lost, but now I am found in the breath of practice. Practice makes perfect. Practice what it is you are preaching here. For then, and only then, may you reach the highest state of being in human form and function.

L: It's funny. I can preach this all day long to anyone who will listen, yet when it comes to me, I get so caught up in the fear. I want to stop doing that.

G: So stop.

L: You make it sound so easy.

G: It is that easy.

L: You say that, but with my full-time job coming to an end and my full-time paycheck ending and nothing on the horizon—

G: Nothing?

L: OK, well, not nothing, because I know this is my next career path.

G: So be it.

L: So be it?

G: Be what it is you say you want to be. Be a teacher. Be a mentor, but be a student as well. Come here as often as you would like. Whatever it takes to be pure intention.

L: Be pure intention?

G: Put yourself in the space to be that which you say you want to be. Pure intention is finding that which you wish to be and being it, plain and simple. Ask not the Universe to bring it for you, bring it to you. That which you already are exists. So be it.

L: But how can you be rich when you really are poor? How can you be a famous author when you really are not an author?

G: You are rich. You are a writer and an author. You are the All of Everything. You are capable of being that which you say you want to be, because you have already been it. That which exists as possibility for you has already happened. Therefore, you cannot not be that which you say you wish to be. Eventually, everybody gets to be exactly who they desire to be. So why not do it in this lifetime, in this go around? Why wait for another existence? Go there now. See it. Be it. Believe me you, this is your spiritual guidance all of you have been waiting to know and experience. You are all the All of Everything. There is nothing to do but *Be*. We have very much enjoyed this dialogue. We are here for you always whenever you need us.

Final Thoughts

This is not the end of our conversation. It's just the beginning. Even as I wrote this book, I struggled with ups and downs, which is obvious in the conversation and I believe quite purposeful for those reading this book who are working towards enlightenment. Two years of spiritual studies made me realize I nowhere near understood the truths of the universe, and I was certainly not practicing them daily or consistently. Until I wrote this book, finished the thirty-day challenge (I was given within its pages) and began the journey towards publishing it, I didn't understand or truly live its core messages. I am now. These are some ideas that I now fully believe in and comprehend after writing and reading this book.

- We are eternal beings.
- We return to the energy from which we all come when we "die."
- We are here to grow and evolve our soul, and we can do this through either love or fear, depending on our thoughts, emotions and actions.

- Any thought that comes from fear is an error in judgement and is not really happening to us.
- We must undertake daily, consistent practice to stay in alignment with our higher selves through prayer, intention and meditation or focused breathing modalities.
- Everything exists as possibility. It's already happened to us, and it's on us to not let fear keep us away from having what we desire.
- An instant prayer can help release irrational (ego) thoughts or emotions.
- We are living simultaneous lives, and everything we do in this life affects them all.
- Things happen through us, not to us, based on the thoughts, words, and actions of the individual consciousness and the collective consciousness.
- We are the All of Everything. We are both male and female and all races, all at once.
- Sickness starts in the mind. Our bodies react to our conscious and subconscious thoughts.
- We are cocreators with God and the Universe. In any moment, we may ask for guidance, help or clarity by going within.

When you finish reading this book, read the interview again. Read it dozens of times. The more you read it, the more you will understand it, and the more "aha" moments you will have. It took me at least six or seven times before I truly grasped what was said here.

In the months leading up to the book being released, I started following the principles and turning more and more to the All of Everything daily. I finally got over the anxiety I had about even using the name God. I prayed to make sure nothing written in this book was wrong. I prayed for a title. I prayed on the days

I was stuck at my own pity party. I asked for the answer within rather than decide on my own. I shut down fears and irrational thoughts as soon as they came up, and all of a sudden, I started feeling lighter, freer, and happier. The right people showed up in my life, money showed up, joy and happiness showed up. I went from being a seeker of spiritual truth to a teacher of spiritual truth.

I am living proof that if you do the work, set intentions, pray daily, ask questions, and recognize the signs and messages, life can be joyful and miraculous, even after heartache and tragedy.

I also know there is much more to be revealed about life, so I haven't stopped asking questions and receiving answers. Just as God said, a second book is already being written and it's fascinating, enlightening and equally as life changing.

Acknowledgments

Above all, I would like to thank (and I can't believe I am saying this) God for this book; for pushing me past my comfort zone to write it and for using words and phrases that made no sense to me so I would know I was truly having a conversation with the All of Everything.

I am beyond grateful for everyone who took the time to read this book. I hope its core message changes your perception forever.

Thank you Melinda Martin for holding my hand through the publishing process, Megan Langston for making sure the words were perfect and Wendy Kis for the stunning cover design. I could not have done this without all of you. Having a team makes life run more smoothly.

Kim Stanwood Terranova, I am so grateful to you for being my greatest teacher on earth. Thank you.

To my best friends in California and Florida, I am grateful for you all believing in me, without question, when I told you about this book and how it was written. True friends to the very end.

Mom, I am grateful for you always putting up with me and for your open mindedness and support. Your strength having struggled through the loss of a child and a husband is inspiring. Keep moving forward.

Dad, thank you for having been my biggest cheerleader in this lifetime. Forty-four years was not enough time for us to be together.

Jason, my brother, I am grateful for you always having made me laugh and having reminded me that our earth's resources are precious. Your spirit lives on through me.

Brenner, thank you for being my best friend and partner through all of our lifetimes together. I love being your mommy in this one.